LIES &
DECEIT

BUT THE FAVOR OF GOD

GUANDER L. GASKIN

HOV
PUBLISHING

Lies & Deceit
But the Favor of God

HOV Publishing a division of HOV, LLC.
www.hovpub.com
hopeofvision@gmail.com

Cover Design: Hope of Vision Designs
Editor/Proofread: Phyllis Bridges for Harvest Seed

Contact the Author, Guander L. Gaskin at:
some1mom5@gmail.com

For further information regarding special discounts on bulk purchases, please visit www.hovpub.com

ISBN Paperback: 978-1-955107-77-8
ISBN eBook: 978-1-955107-76-1

10 9 8 7 6 5 4 3 2 1

Printed in the United States of America

Dedication

I dedicate this book to God the Father and my Lord and
Savior, Jesus Christ.

If it had not been the Lord on my side…

Acknowledgements

My Father God, Lord of Lords, King of Kings, my Savior forever, to You that is holy, righteous, pure, true, and perfect in all Your ways, I give all the thanks, honor, glory, and praise. To You that is, and which was, and is to come, the Holy Father, thank You for choosing me before the foundation of the world and saving me. I thank you for bearing me up on eagle's wings when I could not go on. I thank You for surrounding me with your holy angels, each one busy on assignment on my behalf. Surly, no weapon formed against me prospered.

To my five sons, thank you for giving me a reason to make it another day. Thank you, Ralph, for being my protector and holding your own by God's grace. Thank you, Rod, for your graciousness. Thank you, Marlon, for your sensitivity to the Holy Spirit, your love and protection. Thank you for making a way for us by God's grace when I was almost leveled to the ground. I'm thanking you in advance for all that you will do in the future. My oldest, thank you for the kind, tender-hearted person that you are.

To my baby-boy, Mommy loves you so much. Thank you for all that you have done, especially when I wasn't able to sit up without your assistance. I appreciate your help. I apologize for all the hurt and disruption that you endured during your younger life. Thank you for loving God and believing in Him. You are blessed always, in the name of Jesus.

To my beloved mother, the late Mattie lee Howard, this is a word from my heart. Thank you for bringing me into the world, providing for and protecting me when I could not help myself. Thank you for bringing us to Zion and causing me to be introduced to Holiness. I appreciate you more than you know. Thank you for forgiving me for all the hurt and aggravation I caused in my younger years. Most of all, I walk in freedom because the Most High has forgiven me.

To my sisters, thank you Baby-girl for providing me a place to lay my head during the years of court proceedings. I appreciate you guy's kindness. Thank you, Ernestine, for always being whatever I needed you to be when I needed you.

Thank you, Maw, for your love and kindness. You have no idea how I appreciate you coming through for me. You blessed me when a dime to me was like a ten-dollar bill. Thanks to all my sisters, you all played your part when I was in survival mode.

To the Rams that God placed in the bush for me, you all know who you are, thank you guys for allowing God to lead you. You really stood up in the paint with me when no one else could or would. I thank and appreciate all that the Saints of God have done, from my depth of my heart, thank you.

My Free Life sister, Mary Edwards, thank you for your prayers, Godly wisdom, and love. Thank you for availing yourself during the times when I just needed someone to listen. Thank you for your street smarts. Truly God is a God that wastes nothing; He knew the time would come that I would need your wisdom. Thank you for being a friend and a sister in the Lord.

To my neighbor, Mr. Tommy Smith, (former President of HOA), thank you and the wife for showing me love. There are not words to truly express how it felt to be a stranger in a strange land. You all were the balm to an oozing wound. I appreciate all the help, direction, knowledge, and wisdom you guys graced me with.

To everyone that blessed me financially during the death of my dad, and while going through the demonic court hydra, I cannot thank you enough.

To my Face Book family, (God knows who you are) thank you, thank you.

Thank you, Prayer Warriors, God did it again!

Special Thanks

A very special acknowledgement to Pastor Windle Riles, who truly prayed me through, talked me through, and heard me through. From the days of Mount Hermon, when you were the assistant pastor until now, you were there for me. I love and appreciate you and Sister Riles more than you know. Blessings upon you.

I thank my dad's sister for her untiring prayers, love, and wisdom. I love you, Auntie Alberta.

Thank you, Ms. D for embracing my son just as if he were your own. You never showed any difference in your son and mine. Thank you for all the outings you invited and provided for my son. Your kindness will not go unrewarded. Thank you for every sleepover, meal, and encouraging word you and DeeDee provided.

Last, but never least, to the person that just wanted to do God's will, Rev. Van Shrieves Sr., thank you for your love of God. I appreciate every fiber of your being. Thank you for everything and all things.

Finally, I acknowledge all my enemies, frenemies, liars, switch-outs, and two-faces because it was you all that helped push me to my destiny. I Thank you in a way that you may never understand.

Unapologetically, Guander L. Gaskin

Editor's Message

Editing "Lies & Deceit But The Favor Of God" was a journey for me. Memories that I was sure I had forgotten were recalled. Memories that used to be unpleasant, are now testimonies of what God brought me through and delivered me from. My discussions with the author, Pastor Guander L. Gaskin, revealed her sincere love, faith, and trust in God.

I gained a testimony while working on this book. I was about a third of the way through the editing of the manuscript when my computer suddenly turned off. I gasped in fear of losing my most recent edits. My granddaughter was standing to the side of my computer, which made her think she somehow caused it to shut off. So, she began to apologize profusely. Then it dawned on us that she couldn't have caused it because everything else connected to the surge protector it was plugged into was still on. At first, I was ready to go into panic mode, but as quickly as that feeling tried to overtake me, the peace of God began to sweep over me. Quietly within all I could hear was, 'Settle yourself' repeatedly. As I began to pray, I turned the computer back on. It turned on and loaded with ease as if nothing had happened. I began to search for the manuscript files, but they were not there. Normally, if a computer shuts down improperly, a recovery file is automatically created. Well, much to my surprise I could not find any recovery files for the manuscript. So that you really get the full picture, I had nine files open when the computer suddenly shutdown and only the files for the manuscript were missing! Once I realized this, I understood this was more than a computer issue, but a spiritual matter. With tears in my eyes, I began to call on the name of Jesus. I asked God to illuminate my mind, to show me how to find and recapture the files. As I prayed, again 'Settle yourself' resonated within my spirit. I quietly sat with my eyes closed and slowly it began to come to mind where to look for the files and how to recover them.

Again, of the nine files that were open when my computer failed, only the four files for this book were missing. As I'm writing, the incident makes me think of the title of this book, "Lies & Deceit But The Favor Of God." See, it was a lie designed to deceive and cause a setback, oh but the favor of God prevailed! As you read this book, I pray you will see God's hand of mercy, favor, and ever abounding love. God bless you!

Phyllis Miller-Bridges

Foreword

It is an honorable opportunity to partake in the life journey of one of God's gifted children. One that endured many adversities and is now a dynamic minister of God's Word. She now delights in the old Negro spiritual, "My Soul Looks Back and Wonders How I Got Over."

Come with me, partake of this great experience and journey of endurance and inspiration, and you shall be well pleased for the "Windows of Heaven Shall Pour Out a Blessing."

Dr. Van Xavier Shrieves

Pastor Mt. Zion Baptist Church LaGrange, Georgia

Contents

These events are not in chronological order but are given to you as the Lord recalled them within me.

Chapter 1

Childhood

"Y'all Grandmama told me to pick y'all up," were words we heard daily as my brother and I were picked up and dropped off at home Monday thru Friday after kindergarten. We were sure to be greeted by some stranger in an old, beat-up car that was parked at our house to take us to Mama. My grandmother was the owner of a bar that was known in the sixties as a juke joint, although we called it "The Place". It was my grandmother and granddad's place of business. This is where my brother and I went for a few hours, five days a week until an older family member came to pick us up and take us home. Living in Florida in the sixties, it was safe-to trust most people.

Mama would sit us on the floor behind the bar and give us a coke and a bag of chips. We never thought about the floor being dirty because we loved Mama so much; we were just happy to see her face. Mama was actually my grandmother. We lived in a 3-bedroom, one bath house. The household included my granddaddy, grandmother, five aunts, my mom, my brother and me. In addition, we always had relatives that would come and live at Mama's house until they got on their feet. The house according to records was around 652 sq feet. Although the house was not very big, it was filled with a huge amount of love. My mama was the best and wisest mama you could ever want. I loved her so much! She taught me wisdom that has opened many doors for me and is yet opening doors. You will see what I mean later.

Many of my cousins came to stay with us temporarily until they got on their feet. Most of my cousins from Georgia got their start out of my grandmother's home. Back in the sixties people had love for one another.

I can see me playing in our dirt front yard. Being kids, you'll play with anything, and especially when you are poor, you can get very creative. Just poking sticks in the ground can be entertaining.

I can remember being a little tot running around in my panties. I had a bronze bank made in the torso of Abraham Lincoln. I remember adding every penny I could get my hands on to the bank. In those days, people would come over and give kids a penny or two. Everyone knew T.J. and Lizzie and because of that folks they knew would come over. Some of the people I remember are One-Dime, Big Kid, Zena, King-Size, and Jitterbug. Yes, these are all real people.

I remember when I was six years old, I had a freak accident. One evening after watching cartoons a relative and I went outside to play. There was a garden tool (hoe) lying on the ground and we both wanted it. We began to pull and struggle over it to see who would get it to dig in the ground. The next thing I knew, my head was bleeding. Somehow one of us let go of the hoe, it hit me and split my scalp.

I remember my biological mother changing my panties outside on the bumpy concrete driveway beside my cousin, L.C.'s, car. He was waiting to take me to the hospital. During those days Blacks were not allowed to go to certain hospitals. To get my head stitched up, I was taken to the hospital where only blacks went, known then as Jones Walker. I loved my biological mama so much that I always wanted to be with her. She always kept a few pairs of new panties and an outfit or two for me in case of an emergency or we went to Jacksonville or South Georgia.

About a year later, I remember another incident that happened while we were all outside. I think my granddad was about to go to Jacksonville, Florida. I remember running across the street, but I never made it to the other side. I was hit by a car and thrown up in the air. I was rushed to the hospital; I survived by the grace of God.

Life was good living with Mama. She and my granddad were hard workers and had something to show for their labor. She owned the corner lot across the street, of which she gave a portion to my biological mom to build a house. If I'm not mistaken, we moved into our new home across the street in1969!

After we moved into our new house, we would still sneak over to Mama's house as much as possible. We did this because Mama had a stereo playing the latest black secular artists and my biological mom was in a Pentecostal church. Need I say more? By this time, my biological mom had two girls younger than me. I was the oldest girl even though I was only about eight or nine years old. By default, I was the mama to my two younger sisters. You see, my mother had to work and that's just the way it was back in the day. I loved my siblings very much and would not have wanted it any other way than for me to take care of them myself.

The house my biological mother built had four bedrooms and two baths. I was responsible for keeping the house clean, cooking, washing dishes, bathing my sisters, combing their hair, and getting them dressed for school and bed. I cooked and had to serve everyone. I even had to spoon-feed my younger sisters before I could eat.

My brother and I would get whipped with extension cords or a dry oak switch. I would get a whipping for anything someone said I did, be it a lie or the truth. I was only ten years old and being beaten until my arms were bleeding, swollen and purple, I just couldn't understand why. Now that I'm grown, I've come to think that my mother had a lot of pressure on her that contributed to her actions back then.

Honestly, yes, I got whippings for things I didn't do, but can I just be honest? I also did a lot of things that were worthy of a whipping, but my mom never knew. So, if I tell the truth, it all balanced out!

I was young and had a lot of questions and no one to trust to give me answers. Somehow, I knew there was a God. I knew I was special and believe it or not, I knew I would be saved someday. I didn't know when or how, but I always had thoughts in the back of my mind like… when I get grown if I have a nice house and car…. what about my soul?

I was not popular; I didn't have many friends in elementary school. Looking back, I probably wouldn't have wanted to be my friend because of my attitude and actions. I didn't wear the latest fashions or hair styles, yet I was thankful. I did not have a lot of exposure to people; except for the neighboring kids that attended school with me. I did not have many people, who took the time to talk to me and show me the right road. My grandmother would talk to me but sometimes it seemed more like a curse. When she got frustrated with me, she would repeatedly tell me, "You gone be dead before you are fifteen, you act just like your cousin." I knew Mama loved me dearly and would do anything to get me to act right. For the most part, Mama taught us a lot of things. We were taught how to conduct ourselves in public, not to leave a drink and come back to it, to never go into a place with only one way in and one way out, not to eat any and everybody's cooking because someone may poison you, and if we went into a club, to always sit where we could see everybody coming and going. Her wisdom was priceless and still in fruition today.

I was very bitter as a child. So much responsibility was placed upon me at only ten years old that it made me very bitter. I was also big, and a bit developed for my age, and was often made fun of. Even in places where I felt I should have been safe, I was teased. This did not help my self-esteem at all. At school I was very defiant and would fight without provocation. I'm not proud of the appalling things I said and did. I would disrupt the class, cuss the teacher, and fight any body, anywhere. I remember shoving the principle over into the milk bin.

I cannot say this was a cry for anything, I was just resentful among other things. As I stated earlier, I was a mom by default. I had to come home from school (when I was not suspended) and my daily routine included: cleaning the whole house, cooking, feeding my sisters, washing dishes, bathing my sisters, and getting them ready for bed, combing their hair, and then doing my homework.

My single biological mother, with four children, did the best she could. She worked and Mama helped us out a lot of times. I realized that it can be so easy to be judgmental when you have not gone through what others have dealt with. Now that I'm grown and have experienced raising five children of my own, I have a new perspective.

We were made to go to church, which turned out to be the best thing that ever happened to me and within me. A relative of ours told my biological mother about a Pentecostal preacher and church. We ended up joining this church. That is when Satan turned up the fire. Satan doesn't know everything, but he knows those who are chosen by God. He starts early trying to find an entrance through any door that is opened.

My biological mother did what she felt was right. This included a lot of legalisms. The Pastor of that church was an anointed true Apostle of God. He taught the Word of God with anointing and power as best as he understood. He preached in power and demonstration; I remember seeing miracles, signs, and wonders manifest. I remember a manifestation when he prayed over a handkerchief for my mom. She took the handkerchief to a very sick relative in another state. The handkerchief was laid on the person. The very next day, that person was up and moving around as if she was never sick. This is just one of the manifestations of God's glory that I recall. He would also anoint us with Blessed Oil and pray with the laying on of hands for the people.

Nevertheless, we were not allowed to celebrate holidays, own, or play with baby dolls because Apostle said those things would put a spirit of wanting a baby in a child. I agree with this to a certain point.

We could not have what was referred to as images... baby dolls, statues, animal cookies, and things that were in the shape, form, or image of an animal or man created by God. Now allow me to clarify the animal cookies. There was a deacon that would not allow his children to eat animal crackers. I guess he felt like they were eating images. Some of the deacons drove Mack trucks, which had a bulldog hood handle. Some of them out of ignorance or obedience broke the bulldog off the truck because it was considered an image. Now that I think about it, I wonder how they opened the hood.

We could not listen to secular music. Although I didn't agree as a child, that is exactly the way it should have been. I was but a child when I was taught Joshua 24:15, which says, "As for me and my house, we will serve the Lord." This should be the attitude for every Christian. I have always loved music. Back in the day, we had Isaac Hayes, Isley Brothers, Tyrone Davis, etc. I was not a Christian and was not trying to be, but God had a hold of me even then. I listened to the radio and knew every secular song for blacks and whites. I liked gospel as well. I remember when Mama bought my aunts a floor model stereo and records. I could not stay away from listening to "You're the Best Thing That Ever Happened To Me" and "Midnight Train to Georgia" by Gladys Knight and the Pips.

The sisters and brothers in the church that live right are referred to as Saints or Christians. Acts 11:26b says the disciples were called Christians first at Antioch. A few of the Saints didn't like me, or maybe I just thought so. Now that I'm a child of the Most High God, I realize that it was the Spirit within me that they didn't like. Or was it really me? I just remember a certain sister told my biological mother I was in the street talking to a boy. Well, I may as well have sassed an old person, because even though it was a lie, I got whipped until I could no longer cry. I was left with whelps and bleeding bruises; she would hit you anywhere she could. I have scars on my body today from beatings.

My biological mother would get up in church during testimonial service and announce to the whole church that I got a whipping. This added to my embarrassment and motivated most of the kids to pick on me for months.

I must say, even now, in 2022 there are people that don't know the difference between testifying unto God's glory and tearing up time.

On my way to school one morning, I stopped to speak to the lunchroom manager's older son. He was standing on the corner waiting to catch a cab to work. When the cab arrived, it was driven by my uncle, my mother's brother. I said bye to the guy and continued walking to school.

The school was about seven minutes from the lunchroom manger's home. In less than an hour, I was called to the office. I could not imagine why I was being called to the office to be picked up early; it was not even 10 A.M. My biological mother was there to pick me up and take me home. In that short period of time, my uncle called my mother and told her I was going over to the man's house. What a lie! I was standing on the corner just saying hello. I knew what I was in for when we got home.

There was never any understanding with my biological mom. If you told her something was not the truth, she would say, "Oh, so you're calling a grown person a lie? Grown people don't lie." That was one of the most dreaded rides I ever had in my life. Upon arriving at home, I was told to strip butt naked and get in the bathtub. She beat me so badly. I believe this is when she beat me until she fainted. I was bruised purple and black, and my arms were swollen. This was the absolute worst whipping ever! Then she took me back to school. I'm sure I was not wearing long sleeves. What a day at school!

> *Romans 12:19 says, "Dearly beloved, avenge not yourselves, but rather give place unto wrath: for it is written, Vengeance is mine; I will repay, saith the Lord."*

There are some who hate their parents, family members, or whomever wronged them for doing less than what I experienced and seek revenge on them. In my case, despite what was done to me, the wrongful whipping, and the lie my uncle told on me, which caused me to get the worst whipping of my life, I loved my mother, and I forgave my uncle. Yes, I admit that I was angry and hurt beyond the pain of the whipping. Who wouldn't have hurt feelings and be angry? But all thanks to God, in time my anger subsided, and the hurt began to heal.

God's grace and mercy has always been upon my life. God kept me when I did not understand that I was being kept. I never wished anything bad upon my mother or uncle. Unknowingly, at just twelve years old, God was with me and allowed me to be able to forgive and give it all to Him.

Psalm 105:15 says, "Touch not mine anointed, and do my prophets no harm."

Understand, who God called you to be, who He predestined you to be, you already are… Even at the tender age of twelve, I was already anointed and had the gifts and callings that were upon my life. Gifts and callings are without repentance.

We went to church on Sundays, house-to-house prayer meetings on Mondays, and if I'm not mistaken, to another service during the week. The church was a wooden building with no bathroom or running water. The church officials eventually built two bathrooms and got a water keg.

Sunday school was from 10 a.m. to 11 a.m., church service was from 11:15 a.m. until the testifying, singing, and preaching was finally finished. This was normally somewhere between 3 p.m. and 3:30 p.m. Sunday evenings we went back to church for night service from 6 p.m. until 11 p.m.

All the time, God was working strategically, getting me ready for the call that He placed upon my life. He was building my spiritual stamina. God truly is Alpha and Omega; He knows us better than we know ourselves. God is always in control.

Our Pastor lived about two hours away in another city. I hated going to church. Even though, I hated going, I was listening. I was being poured into. As I said earlier, the Pastor taught as best as he understood. He was a powerful, anointed preacher that walked in authority. He was a straight shooter; he gave you the Word of God blood raw, with no compromise. To this very day, I thank God for the Man of God. Had my biological mother not made me go to church I would not be where I'm today.

That church was my spiritual foundation. Although I didn't understand why my life seemed so hard; God had it all in control.

Jeremiah 29:11 says, "For I know the thoughts that I think toward you, saith the LORD, thoughts of peace, and not of evil, to give you an expected end."

Chapter 2

Rebellious

In the year of 1972, church was pretty much the highlight of the week. We would choose a boyfriend in church (you know we had to sneak). We passed notes while the preaching was going on and laughed at the way certain saints looked while they were doing the Holy dance or testifying. It seemed so foreign to us as children. Our parents would trust us to go to another saint's house to play with their kids. It was exciting and we enjoyed it for the most part. We were all young, ranging in age from eleven to fifteen years old. I never did drugs, drank alcohol, or smoked. I didn't like school clubs or the dances that were held at the recreation center every weekend. Plus, it wasn't like we were allowed to go anyway. Although some of the saint's kids would sneak and go, my name wasn't on that list, and it didn't need to be. I was fast and fine; I didn't need to be anywhere else at night but home or church. God was covering me, and I didn't realize it.

By the time I was twelve, I felt I had enough. I devised a plan to run away. That night, when everyone was asleep, I packed some clothes and left through my bedroom window. There was a teacher that was cool with me and new to the neighborhood. I went to his house at 2:00 a.m. I asked him to take me to my friend's house, which he did and that's where I stayed that night. I was living moment by moment.

When daylight came, I knew it was apparent that I ran away from home. At this point in time, your parents would be in one of two states of mind; you were going to get the killing of your life, or they were glad you were safe. In my case, I was not taking any chances; I hung around anywhere I could during the day.

I was not a clubber, of course, I was only twelve years old. However, I went to Pinders (a club where elderly people hung out). The female bartender said to me, "The police have been here with your picture, looking for you; be careful." I thanked her but did not leave immediately.

I don't recall exactly how it all happened. I remember, I began to talk with this deputy, who was on duty patrolling outside of the club. I don't know why, but somehow, we got into a conversation. For reasons unknown, he allowed me to stay at his house. He treated me with kindness and respect. He never tried to get fresh or make any sexual advances toward me. Looking back at this situation, I realize it was by divine appointment; God's love and protection provided me safe shelter. He let a couple of his coworkers know that I was there. Can you imagine? I'm on the runaway list and the deputy is hiding me out! God's tender mercy and the prayers of the saints trumped what the devil planned. I could have easily fallen into the hands of someone who could have abused and harmed me badly, or even taken my life, but God was with me! For that I will forever be grateful!

After a while, I went back to my biological mom's house. Some of my relatives were glad to see me and others were glad I had been away. After it was discovered that the deputies were privy to my runaway, they were relieved of their duties. Needless to say, it made the news and local headlines.

After this happened, my biological mom turned me over into the hands of the Lord. She had given me all that she could and had raised and taught me as best as she knew how and believed. Ultimately, she gave me to God.

Despite all the things that happened, way back in the corners of my mind, I always knew I would be saved and in ministry someday. I cannot tell you how I knew, but I knew it without a shadow of doubt.

There was a nursing home located not too far from where we lived. It was converted into Clemente Park. A lot of people went there to hang out and shoot basketball. There were swings for the kids and a community library. One evening, I decided to walk to the park. I never thought for a moment that a five-minute walk would take me 37 years to complete. Keep reading, you will eventually understand what I mean.

After being at the park a few minutes, my cousin and her boyfriend pulled up in their car. I spoke to her, and she asked me if I wanted to ride with them. I said yes and got in the car. We rode a bit and ended up at their place. While I was there, the best friend of my cousin's boyfriend came by. She introduced us and after a few times of going to my cousin's place and seeing this person there, I began to refer to him as boyfriend, which lead to him becoming my boyfriend.

Jeremiah 1:5 says, "Before I formed thee in the belly, I knew thee; and before thou camest forth out of the womb I sanctified thee, and I ordained thee a prophet unto the nations."

God is all knowing, he knows our birth date, he knows our death date, He knew us before we were born, and ordained us.

Chapter 3

Boyfriend

As time went on, I saw Boyfriend about five nights a week. Let me make this clear, I didn't like him as a boyfriend in the beginning. He was what I considered overweight, and he had big, flat, wide feet. Besides that, he already had a girlfriend; but for whatever the reason, they soon broke up.

I was young, unlearned, and foolish. He worked at a dealership and had a nice canary yellow car with a vinyl top, eight track tape system, and nice cloth seats. After he got off work, he would go home, get dressed and then come pick me up. We would ride around and maybe go out for ice cream.

When Mama found out who Boyfriend's parents were, she hit the roof! Understand this, Mama was old school, and she gave us so much wisdom. She taught us about things that I thought would never be necessary for the day that we lived in. Please know, I now walk in the wisdom that I was taught.

Mama told me that she knew his parents, and that his daddy's girlfriend lived on the same street as she did. She told me that his dad was abusive and had a lot of women and outside children. She begged me to leave Boyfriend alone. I heard the same information from other older people that I came across. I was warned about a lot of things that I would not have suffered, had I just listened. Being young, I turned a deaf ear to everything that I was told about Boyfriend and his family. I began to like Boyfriend, though to this day, I cannot imagine why.

One night, me, Boyfriend, my cousin, and her boyfriend were riding in the car. I got out of the car and mistakenly closed the door on my cousin boyfriend's hand. That man cussed me out so badly, and Boyfriend in no way defended me. That alone was a red light and warning sign, at least it should have been to me.

It seemed like Boyfriend could not get off work soon enough, go get cleaned up and come pick me up. Some Friday nights we went to the drive-in theatre. Sometimes, I gladly took my two younger sisters with us. Even until this very day, they have not forgotten it, which makes me smile.

A neighbor, who knew Boyfriend, asked me why he parked his car around the corner after dropping me off at night. I asked her if she was sure. She said, "Yes," and told me, "The next time he drops you off at night, check it out." I did just what she said, and to make a long story short, to my surprise, he was in modern day terms, stalking me. One night, I was talking to a deputy friend of the family. After chatting for about ten to fifteen minutes, he left. I was only a few feet from the yard. As I turned to walk home, I heard someone call my name. I continued to walk because I thought I was just hearing things. I heard my name again. Now, I was sure someone called me; I turned around and saw that it was Boyfriend. As he was walking swiftly toward me, he was saying, "What are you doing talking to that N?" Before I could answer, he hit me so hard! It was funny and unbelievable all at the same time. I was laughing while trying to explain. What I should have been doing was swinging on him! Being naive and unlearned, I didn't realize that this was a red flag to leave him alone. He apologized for his behavior, sometimes crying and I forgave him.

In another incident, I was with my cousin at Sable Palms Apartments, and it was getting late. So, my cousin asked her stepbrother to take me home. He was not old enough to have a permit or license. He was maybe fourteen years old. Again, I heard my name being called. I turned around and it was a repeat of the last time. He hit me so hard and then he ran. This time I was not laughing. I would have fought him that night, but he got away.

The day came when Boyfriend took me home to his parents' house. He lived with his parents. The house had a carport that sheltered cars, motorcycles, and dogs. It was confusing trying to distinguish the front from the side or back. After making my way through everything stored under the carport, there were two doors. A wooden screen door that led to the kitchen, and a sliding glass door that led to his dad's private part of the house, which was just a room. I was introduced to his mother, a very sweet and kind person. The dad, in my opinion, was not a warm person! How did I know he didn't like me? Well, the dad had a problem with me because I never felt like laying in the road for anyone. I wasn't going to take your mess or bend over backwards for you. He told his son, I was bossy, and if it were him, he would not take that from me. From day one of meeting me, to the day he checked out, he never liked me.

Later, I found out there was a feud between Boyfriend's dad and my granddad. Boyfriend's parents lived about a five-minute walking distance from my grandparents. My granddad explained the situation to me. My uncle hit an old, useless, undrivable junk truck that belonged to Boyfriend's dad. Although, my uncle drank on the weekends, he held down a decent job during the week for years. Because of this, Boyfriend's dad demanded that my uncle pay him for hitting the truck. He even had the nerve to follow him home to get the money. Because my uncle had been drinking; he had no option but to pay him. I'm sure he didn't want any issues with the law and drunk driving. That explains why my uncle locked the gate when Boyfriend's car was parked on my uncle's property.

As time passed, we moved in together. I was about seventeen years old at this time. Boyfriend rented a little house where the landlord lived next door. At that time, I didn't have any children, so it was just me and him. He had friends that would stop by and smoke a little weed with him. As I said earlier, I didn't do drugs, weed or alcohol. Boyfriend was five years older than me. He kept a job and wanted to have something in life. This was definitely a plus for me. There were times when he would get angry and physically abuse me. This dude forever accused me of being with other men.

As I write this book, I can't help but think, had I known then what I know now, I would have done things so differently. I praise God for Grace and Mercy! All these things were a sure sign of trouble ahead!

He would jump on me or hit me because at that time, I wouldn't fight him back. However, there is never a justifiable reason for abuse. While fighting me, you could see a demonic force within him. Although I was not a Christian at the time, I knew another personality would take charge of him; there was someone else in there. At that time, I was not as knowledgeable about demonic forces as I am now.

One time, a cousin was over, and he got upset about something. He jumped on me and punched me. I fell to the floor, and he kicked me for a few times. My cousin told my mother what happened. (I found out later that he was fooling around with the cousin.) My mother went to see him at his job about the incident; although there was no way he would have admitted what he did. I believe my mama would have rocked his world. Strangely, I have never known him to fight anyone other than me.

I became pregnant with our first child while we were living in the little house. He wanted us to have our own house, so he began to look for a house. Boyfriend wanted something in life, and he was a hard worker. He qualified to get a new government subsidized house. He told me to choose which house I wanted, and I did. He always included me in the decision making when choosing a car, house, etc. I cannot take that away from him. He was a good provider, but just stingy. He never did right by me with money.

We took trips and did things that most people our age, and even older, had not. I remember back in the day, we went to Dallas, Texas. While there we went to the house where television series "Dallas" was filmed. I can't throw the baby out with the bath water; Boyfriend showed me some good times.

In 1977, we moved into a brand-new block house. I lived there from '77 to 2009. At the time, the only furniture we had was a bed that we bought from a used furnishing store, and a used stove and fridge. I was thankful to have a new house and appreciated the little we had. Later, we bought a yellow, plastic étagère (shelf) that I took apart and used for various purposes.

We borrowed a small black and white TV from his dad. We ate our meals sitting on the side of the bed until we could afford to do better. He always paid the bills and kept transportation for me. There were some good times. On Friday nights, we would put the mattress on the floor and watch TV. Sometimes, we would go get a burger or ride out of town. Overall, he was a decent person until he was in the company of a relative that had control over him, or that fighting demonic force took over him.

I can only recall riding the bus twice ever in my lifetime. Boyfriend always provided me transportation to my prenatal appointments. He was excited about the baby! He told his family and friends that we had a baby on the way.

We planned to have our baby at the midwife's house because it was cheaper. Boyfriend suggested this because I didn't have any health insurance, but neither did most of the young mothers. I didn't think about all the women that had babies at the hospital, who did not have any insurance.

One day, nearing my nineth month, I was lying in the bed, but when I stood up, I thought I was urinating without any control. Then I realized that my water had broken. Would you believe this man almost cussed me out? All I could do was take it; because at this point my only concern was having our baby. Plus, I had no control over my water breaking. I honestly think that he was just nervous and excited all at the same time. He wiped the floor up and took me to the midwife. I gave birth to our first son without any complications. The midwife was everything we needed her to be. Boyfriend was so excited!

A few months later, I was pregnant again. I gave birth to our second son. Taking care of two babies was a full-time job. Boyfriend made sure they had what they needed, as best as he could. When the boys were old enough, I began to work here and there. Again, I just knew that one day, I would be saved and preaching to the nations. Isn't it funny how through all phases of my life, I could not shake off Jesus? I really don't think I wanted to.

I remember us visiting one of his relatives, who lived near Tampa, Florida. During the visit, his relative and I had a disagreement, which became heated. It didn't matter to me that this relative attended medical school. I refused to allow him or anyone else to talk down to me. Especially, knowing the many times that he and Boyfriend smoked marijuana at our house; I was not the one to be disrespected. It really didn't matter that we were at his house. Again, Boyfriend did nothing in my defense. I could never figure out why Boyfriend was so controlled by this relative. To this very day, nothing has changed.

Of course, I was ready to leave now, which made Boyfriend very angry with me. Would you believe he drove 113 miles to take me home? This was one of the most miserable trips of my life. The man cussed me out all the way home, and even spit in my face, then dropped me off at home.

I didn't realize it then, but God was truly helping me. Reader, come on now, you would have never allowed that, and normally I wouldn't have either. Spitting in someone's face is the lowest form of disrespect! It was about 2:00 a.m. when we arrived at our house. I got out of the car and took the baby with me. Before I could get in the house, he backed out of the driveway and headed back to St. Petersburg, Florida. That relative has always had control over Boyfriend. Maybe his being in the medical field had some type of persuasion over him. To this day, I cannot figure it out.

One day while out and about, a woman said to me, "Your husband was trying to talk to me." Meaning, he was getting fresh with her. We were not married at the time. I said, "Are you sure?" She replied, "He was in that white truck with your two babies." The woman stated she was not interested in him. Finding this out really hurt me. I just wanted to have my family and be happy.

Looking back, I was as my grandmother used to say, "green as gall." I should have left. However, I couldn't because God was in control. Also, had I done that, I would not be writing this book because none of what you will read in the later chapters would have happened. God is sovereign, He is in control.

After working at the car rental agency for ten years, Boyfriend decided to become self-employed. He opened his first body shop on the corner of Seaboard and Michigan Ave. It was small and located in the back. He did more simonizing than painting. Boyfriend never gave me money or told me how much he made per day or weekly. He paid the bills, but he was very stingy. Because I was young and naïve, I didn't demand that he allow me to manage the finances. He took advantage of that fact.

How you start out with a person is how you will end, unless God is allowed in. He would fix certain women's cars, without charging any money. Oh, but it wasn't free. Of course, he worked for money, but the other was a private barter between him and the woman. I look back and think, 'why did I put up with all that madness?' I had to because it was in the permissive will of God. God is sovereign, He is always in charge. Had I done otherwise, my story would different.

As usual, I was home taking care of our children, while he was out. I truly loved Boyfriend and wanted love reciprocated. I wanted us to be happy and comfortable together. I don't know of a hurt that cuts deeper or aches as badly as when the person you love and trust hurts you. I really loved him and wanted to live happily ever after with him. At the time, I could never have imagined that in the years to come, I would hate the day I ever went to the park, which set into motion us meeting. Happily ever after, only happens in fairytales or where God reigns.

I've always loved having nice things and decorating. When I became financially able, I bought nice things for the house to make him comfortable. I have always put me on the back burner to make others happy. I was young and a good mother. I kept my house in order and my children clean. I cooked wholesome meals for my family and enjoyed it.

Early on, it became apparent that the burden was on me to protect me and my family. But how can this be? When God said that the head of every woman is the man? It only works the way God said when Christ is the head of every man. To this very day, I cannot stand a weak man! I'm so glad fear was not in my DNA.

Once, a friend of his went to jail, and to raise bail money, his mom sold his nice floor model television to Boyfriend. When the person was released from jail, he told him he wanted his television back. Would you believe this man told him that I bought the television, and he would have to talk to me? He could have told him that he wasn't going to sell the television back to him. His friend knew better than to confront me about that television. The bigger television was a blessing to my house. I was tired of watching that small, borrowed, black and white television.

Looking at the big picture, I was not appreciated by him or loved. I don't think he turned down anything but his collar. Nevertheless, I was pregnant again with our third child. This would make three boys. I could never understand why he never rushed home to be with his family. The house was clean, magazine decorated, children taken care of, and dinner ready. A nice meal, not sausage and pork and beans, but what some would call a Sunday dinner. A real shame that it took me 37 years to figure out why the man took his time coming home.

Despite all that was taking place, I knew God had a calling on my life and I would one day go before the nations. (UNDERSTAND WHAT YOU GO THROUGH, DEPENDS ON

HOW GOD IS GOING TO USE YOU. THE GREATER THE ANOINTING ON YOUR LIFE, THE HIGHER THE COST.)

Eventually, after a few years, we were married. I noticed a change in my husband's demeanor and behavior for the better. He was so kind to the boys. I knew something major was going on. Y'all the man repented, got baptized and got saved!

It didn't take me long to see the hand of God working in power and demonstration within him. He began to attend service at a Pentecostal church. This is the type of church that I grew up in church. The family would go to church with him, but I was not saved.

After a few years, I divorced my husband, but not according to biblical principles. I promised God, I would not divorce him except it be for adultery. I was not saved, and the devil wasn't either! When he accepted Christ, the devil hired me. I wanted to be single and free to do what I never got a chance to. Or so, I thought.

How many people know that God will Baker Act you? The Baker Act is a Florida law that enables families and loved ones to provide emergency mental health services and temporary detention for people who are impaired because of their mental illness, and who are unable to determine their needs for treatment.

Basically, the Baker Act provides protection against a person's will, but it's what's best for them. I didn't want it, but God knew what was best for me. He provided the protection I needed. When I look back now, I'm so grateful!

Everything I tried to get into, God blocked it. I mean every single thing, He blocked it! I wanted so badly to tell God to just leave me alone. I felt like, He let other people do what they wanted; so why do You keep messing up everything for me? I was aggravated with God because He kept me from what only He truly knows. (What is not written in the Book of Life will not happen.)

My life began to take a downward spiral. I wanted my husband back; but he was not thinking about getting back with me. This makes me think of the children of Israel and how that they complained because they wanted meat. God gave them what they wanted, but it came with a cost. They got so sick, even to point of it coming out of their nose. You can read about this in Numbers 11:18-20. Sometimes we should let well enough, be enough for us. My husband was angry, embarrassed, and hurt, which was enough, but there were also naysayers whispering in his ear.

All I can tell you is this, God beat the hell out of me, and I do mean literally. When, God turned me a loose, I repented, got saved, and was filled with the Holy Ghost. All of this happened at home. There was no one standing over me telling me to call on the name of Jesus. What was so amazing, I didn't have to tell anyone that I had made a change in my life; they told me.

That took place many years ago, I'm yet spirit filled and have been for over 39 years. When you allow God to change your ways, God will change His toward you. That part of my life was very difficult and so deep.

John 4:4 says, "And he must needs go through Samaria." Just as it was ordained by God for Jesus to go through Samaria while in route to Galilee, God ordained my path. Jesus needed to go through Samaria to get to his destination so that the will of God could be accomplished. I needed to go through all that I went through to get to my destination so that the will of God could be accomplished within me.

Chapter 4

Junk Church

Now, we both attended the Pentecostal church where I grew up. The original leader from my childhood passed in the early '70's. He was an Apostle in word and deed, a very kind, no nonsense, Holy Ghost filled man of God. However, you can only teach what you know or have been taught. There were some things that he taught and enforced that were not sound scripturally, which could have been condemned. Titus 2:8 says, "Sound speech, that cannot be condemned; that he that is of the contrary part may be ashamed, having no evil thing to say of you."

I want to make this crystal clear; I would rather kill flesh than to appease it. We were kids, so not celebrating holidays or participating in certain things because of how we were being taught in church didn't kill or take anything away from us. We were taught that it was a sin to celebrate holidays. We could not have baby dolls, or anything made in the likeness of a living thing (it was referred to as an image). The boys that played football were not allowed to go to football banquets, nor birthday parties, and there was no exchanging of gifts at school at Christmas time. We were taught against eating the foods that were cooked on holidays, because according to their understanding it was offered as food sacrificed to idols. So, there was no Christmas dinner, no Thanksgiving Dinner, etc. Now, I know better; however, back then it was not really a problem for me. I would rather do certain things with restraints than be too loose.

After Apostle Dan went to be with the Lord, the lot fell to a certain man, who was either a deacon or an elder. Now we had a new pastor. To this day, I cannot understand how the hierarchy was so out of order because we had a bishop, and it was his job to appoint the new pastor. The new pastor was married and had four children. I know people will be people and to this day there are some who idolize pastors and their family; even their grandchildren are placed on a pedestal.

For the most part, the new pastor was a man of God. He was kind and at times a man of wisdom. He has been a blessing to many people in many ways. However, in my opinion there was also a questionable side of him. Please understand, I in no way or form desire to speak lies or negatively about anyone. However, I witnessed things that I never want to happen to anyone. There are always people that will do whatever is necessary to be in the click or the club. This became prevalent there with some of the people. Even though this was common there and is in many churches, there will always be a remnant who wants what is right and is willing to stand alone for what is right. Now, I truly understand that fact.

Monday night was prayer meeting. It was not prayer meeting as most people know it to be. Many times, the pastor would not be there. He said, "I done been faithful." So, most of the time he was not there. Sometimes it was so rough that I dreaded going. You just never knew what was going to happen or who would be roasted that night.

If a person had a scripture or question, they could bring it to the floor for discussion. There was a deacon that studied to show himself approved, who would hold the discussions accountable to the word of God. I need not tell you that he was not popular; because you never are when you go against the grain. This deacon would not just throw out an answer, he studied and prayed about it so that the next time he saw you, he could give you sound biblical answers.

One Monday night during prayer meeting, the subject was divorce. Being that the pastor's daughters were divorced and remarried; you can see how this could be extremely debatable. Now I'm saved, but my husband and I are not together. He is still running the auto body and repair shop that we have had for years.

There was this one woman that liked him; she worked with the pastor's daughter-in-law. I would occasionally go to the shop because we had children, and when I had a reason. He would be nice to the children but nasty towards me. He would come to my house to pick the children up for church, but he would not give or offer me a ride. Remember, we went to the same church. After he picked up the kids, I would lock the door and walk to the corner where drugs were sold, and someone there would give me a ride to church. The dope crew, folks who weren't saved gave me a ride to church.

The pastor's wife gave an oration saying that the members should ride to church with the one that lived closest to them. This is why we should be kind to everyone. God said for us to love our neighbor as ourselves. (Read Mark 12:31)

You never know who you will need. My car had burned up, so at the time I didn't have a car. He had an extra vehicle, a station wagon, that he loaned to a guy in the church for him and his family.

I remember catching a ride to church and not having a way home. So, I asked one of the saints that lived in my same subdivision if I could catch a ride home. He declined giving me a ride and told me he was going to stop by the store. I lived about six miles from the church in a rural area that was along a stretch of dark highway. I was so angry! I started walking; I was mad enough to not care. Someone picked me up and gave me a ride home. Later, his wife told me that she didn't allow him to ride women when she wasn't in the car.

Getting back to the woman that wanted to be with my ex-husband. She would go to the shop and stand around talking to him for hours. She drove an old Mercedes and worked for the school system with the pastor's daughter-in-law. They both lived in Fort Myers Shores subdivision. One day, while passing through the subdivision, I saw the woman. I stopped my car and got out; she ran into the house. I threw something at her! Honestly that was it!

During the Sunday service announcements, my ex-husband and I were asked to remain at church after service. When the congregation left, in addition to us, six men remained. Two of them were deacons and the others were just random guys asked to stay. They knew what was going on, but we had no idea at all!

The supposed deacon (the pastor's son-in-law) said to me, "Didn't we tell you we were going to give you your papers if you started that foolishness?" I felt like I was in the twilight zone! I had no idea what he was talking about. As far as I knew, he didn't have that type of authority.

I asked, "What are you talking about?" He said, "You went over to that woman's house and cussed her out and someone had to get you out of the road because you were raising sand." I was thinking, is this real... I said, "That is a lie, what are you talking about?" He replied, "Why would that woman lie on you?" I said, "The same reason Jeffery Dahmer killed those kids, the devil! I was so hurt that these guys, most of whom I grew up with, would believe a sinner, a woman out of the streets that they didn't even know over me. It cut like a knife, and a dull one at that. The head honcho doing all the talking was the pastor's son-in-law. I told him, "Save the letter, I'm gone." He wasn't even a Christian. Despite him having done me wrong, I felt so bad for my husband, they threatened to put him out of the church as well. It was all just so messed up! As I said, I have seen so much injustice allowed in the church. My wound was deep because my own put me out of the church that I grew up in and supported with my time and finance.

The Word teaches us in Acts 6:1-7 that the deacons were appointed because the widows were being neglected. Their position came with specific requirements, they had to be honest, full of the Holy Ghost and wise.

They put me out of the church, or you can say, I left voluntarily. I know enough not to rejoice over iniquity. I walked out of the church with no plans of looking back. As for my six accusers: one is currently in prison for pedophilia; two are deceased, one of whom had a massive heart attack and died enroute to the hospital; there's one with severe health problems; another divorced and married his ex-wife's niece; and the other one left the church and is back out in the world serving Satan.

Let's go to Word of God…

Psalm 55:12-15 says, "For it was not an enemy that reproached me; then I could have borne it: neither was it he that hated me that did magnify himself against me; then I would have hid myself from him: But it was thou, a man mine equal, my guide, and mine acquaintance. We took sweet counsel together, and walked unto the house of God in company. Let death seize upon them, and let them go down quick into hell: for wickedness is in their dwellings, and among them."

Understand, I am in no way saying that the things which happened to my accusers was because of the judgment I received from them.

This scripture resounds in my spirit, "Touch not mine anointed, and do my prophets no harm." 1 Chronicles 16:22

Some of the sisters from the church called me and suggested that I ask the deacon for a meeting to see if I could come back to the church. Although, I didn't want to, I asked for a meeting. This time Deacon Albert and Deacon Ellis, the two elderly deacons with wisdom, were there.

Most of congregation knew nothing about me being put out of church until later. Pastor said he didn't know, until my uncle went over to his house to ask him about it. To this very day, I have a problem believing Pastor really didn't know, especially given the type of man he was and the authority that he operated under. I can't see anyone disrespecting his leadership and authority that much. God knows the truth.

During the second meeting, the pastor's son-in-law asked, "How do we know you aren't going to do it again? One of the older deacons countered him with, "How do any of us know what we are going to do?" So, I was allowed to come back to church. Honestly, me leaving the church for those months was a blessing, my eyes were opened. Eventually, I left this church for good; I wasn't growing there anymore. My season on Carver Street was over.

As time went on, I became pregnant with my fourth child. The sisters at the church gave me a very nice baby shower. That was the first time ever that I remember anyone doing anything that nice for me. I never received anything special from my husband. As a matter of fact, in all the years we were together he never bought me a wedding ring. That's right, not even one from the pawn shop. I never demanded one either, because I didn't know any better. You see, all that time I thought the man didn't know any better, but years down the road, I realized I was being played. Even in that, God was faithful. Spiritually, it was like when Jesus told the woman at the well, that she has had five husbands and the one she currently had was not her husband. The Holy Ghost revealed to me that he was not my husband. Yes, by law we were married, but spiritually this was not a marriage ordained by God.

(To learn more about the woman at the well, please read John 4:5-29)

My fourth baby was another boy. He was so handsome and still is to this day. I heard one of the church mothers say when she was carrying her babies, she prayed over them. So, I did likewise. It really made a difference; it worked for me. Not only was he a handsome baby, but the favor of God has always been upon his life. He was never any trouble in church, school, or at home; he was an obedient child. Listen, when I decided to move to the suburbs of Atlanta, Georgia, he chose to make that transition with me. God has blessed him abundantly; he was hired at a fortune 500 company on the spot! Not long thereafter, he met and married a wonderful, educated young lady from a Christian home. Neither of them had children before marriage. Okay, now I'm getting ahead of myself, but God is so faithful. To this very day goodness and mercy is yet following him. As you continue to read, you will see what I mean.

As I mentioned earlier, the Monday night prayer meetings were basically a roast and sometimes it was so rough that I dreaded going. There was a group of church members who caused mass confusion. Remember, Pastor did not attend most prayer services, so many times what was discussed there would be taken to him in a way that it was not said or intended.

Some began to nitpick on my husband so badly that he left the congregation. The devil was waiting with welcoming arms to receive him.

Upon his leaving, an unsaved person recommended him going to a certain movement whose doctrine stated...

1. They are the only church you will find in the Bible.

2. Women are not supposed to speak in church.

3. No instruments are allowed in church.

4. Paul was the last Apostle.

5. There is no such thing as the Holy Ghost.

6. There are no more miracles being performed today.

7. A woman cannot pray if a man is present.

These are just a few of their beliefs. I didn't know of the erroneous teaching until later. So, he joined this movement, which of course wanted him to think that they loved him so much. Everything was brother this and that. I didn't agree with their doctrine, it was not biblical, and in my opinion was just plain crazy.

This led to arguments about him taking the boys to church with him. I knew the man was to be the head of the house, amen. However, the scripture says in Galatians 1:9, "If any man preach any other gospel unto you than that ye have received, let him be accursed." I was not about to sit back and allow my children to be infused with demons and erroneous teaching. This brought about a separation in the household. Nevertheless, I stood with the Word of God, which says in Acts 5:29, "Then Peter and the other apostles answered and said, We ought to obey God rather than men."

Chapter 5

Harlem Lake

After my exodus from Carver Street, I went to visit my cousin's church, which was located in a drug infested, run down subdivision known as Harlem Lake. I grew up around there, so I was not afraid. As a matter of fact, to this day, I have quite a few relatives that reside there. I had some of my best childhood days in aka The Lake. Little did I know, I would end up staying ten years at the Apostolic Church. I always loved the way my cousin loved the Lord and how she had faith in Him, unwavering faith. My cousin was a woman of God and a mighty prayer warrior. Just to hear her talk about the Lord made me want Him more. You could call her any time; day or night and she would pray for you.

I remember when this young lady called me crying. She told me that the police had her brother surrounded in the house and they were going to kill him. She told me that she immediately fell on her knees and begged them not to kill her brother. The police still told her that they were going to kill him. I immediately gathered my purse, cell phone and car keys. My husband asked me where I was going, and I told him what was going on. He told me that I should not go over there and get involved in that matter. It was my Christian duty to help others and who can tell what God is doing?

I asked the young lady for her address and told her, "Ain't nobody killing nobody, in Jesus Name!" She lived about seven to ten minutes from me. I called my prayer warrior cousin and told her what was going on. She told me that she already knew, and that she heard a helicopter. One of us said, "Lets pray!" And that is just what we did!

For where two or three are gathered in my name, there am I in the midst of them. Matthew 18:20

Upon my arrival, there were cars, people looking and the police helicopter hovering over the house using infra-red rays. I parked in front of the house. We began to pray and bind the devil. In about ten to fifteen minutes, the young lady that called me about her brother walked over to my car and whispered... "He's gone." I asked, "Who is gone?" She said, "My brother, God gave him what to do." She told me that he got into a cold shower so that the infrared could not detect him. Then he put on lady's clothing, walked out the door and mingled with the people. The Most Holy God blinded and bound the policemen. The young man eventually eased around the corner to where a car was waiting for him. God did it again! Yes, the young man was about that life, fast illegal megabucks. No! I do not condone that life. I was looking at the fact that he has a soul, and he was somebody's child. Also, despite his lifestyle, he was always very respectable to me. I'm reminded of God's unwavering love, which gave Jezebel a space to repent.

That's the kind of faith our pastor taught. She instilled and drilled faith in God's Word in power and demonstrated that strength to all that knew her.

Pastor, who was endearingly referred to as Mother, would often tell of signs, wonders, and miracles that God had done for her or some of the saints in the church. I recall her reminiscing about the time when one of the saints died and was in the morgue. Mother went in and called her name and she answered.

Matthew 10:8 says, "Heal the sick, cleanse the lepers, raise the dead, cast out devils: freely ye have received, freely give."

Pastor had a double portion anointing upon her life such as I had never seen and may never see again. She was refined, but at the same time approachable. She could speak a thing and rarely did her words fall to the ground. She warned a member not to leave Florida to do mischief to another person. She told him if he left the state of Florida, he would not make it back. The brother was killed in an accident before he could cross the Florida state line. Another time, she told one of the saints they would be a millionaire. Sure enough, it came to pass. These are just a few things; I could go on and on. She was a woman of standards and demanded Holiness unto the Lord. I referred to her as my cousin's pastor, but I became a member of the church as well.

Mother was lead of the Lord to relocate to Florida though she had a home in the Midwest. God gave her a vision of a place with palm trees. Most of the members of the church were from the Midwest as well. Many of them had been under her leadership from their childhood. She pushed education and most of the saints had degrees and decent jobs. I had never seen such a woman of faith and radicalness. We were taught, if it has been done by a human, it can be done by you. Mother was very positive and advocated for education and doing things with quality and excellence.

Church was always incredible! You just never knew what the Lord was going to do or who He would use to do it. Mother pushed receiving the gift of the Holy Ghost. She believed in what some call tarrying. To tarry means to wait. Saints of old would have you on your knees praying and calling on the name of Jesus or saying, "Thank You Jesus," over and over, waiting for the Holy Ghost to come in. Which was not bad, because when you have been on your knees for a while, you begin to focus on God. I truly think that was the sole purpose of it. Once you focused on God, you didn't care about the snot or tears, you just wanted the Holy Ghost. I can tell you it works! However, that is not the only way or place you can receive the Holy Ghost. When your heart is right, the Holy Ghost will fall on you washing dishes, sitting down, at your bedside, or just wherever you may be at God's appointed time. But you must repent and be baptized for the remission of your sins as it says in Acts 2:38. Some speak in a heavenly language known as tongues, which is a gift also. One thing about the Holy Ghost; you don't have to tell people. They will tell you.

Acts 2:1- 4 says, "And when the day of Pentecost was fully come, they were all with one accord in one place. And suddenly there came a sound from heaven as of a rushing mighty wind, and it filled all the house where they were sitting. And there appeared unto them cloven tongues like as of fire, and it sat upon each of them. And they were all filled with the Holy Ghost, and began to speak with other tongues, as the Spirit gave them utterance."

Mother taught us that you can ask God for anything and if you have faith, He will do it. I have put this into action so many times. She taught us about the Power of the Blood of Jesus… How you can be in a situation and call on the Blood of Jesus and by faith the power in the Blood and name of Jesus really works and moves in your situation. You must have faith!

Matthew 21:22 says, "And all things, whatsoever ye shall ask in prayer, believing, ye shall receive."

Psalm 46:1 says, "God is our refuge and our strength, A very present help in trouble."

Jesus is the name above all names. At the name of Jesus every knee shall bow and every tongue shall confess that He is Lord. The almighty name of Jesus alone can cancel the devil's agenda!

I remember being in the Midwest at a church event. As I got out of the car onto a four-lane street, walking half asleep across the street, I misjudged the timing of an approaching vehicle. Three of the saints were on the other side of the road talking. I heard a sister yell, "THE BLOOD OF JESUS!" I immediately fell into a pile of leaves, only to find out I had come so close to getting hit by the car! The man driving the car thought he had hit me. Oh, but the Blood covered me!

Not long after, I began singing in the choir and from there Mother nominated me to the office of Missionary President. I absolutely love Ministry. I knew God was telling me to step out into my calling. During a Sunday service, Mother called me up and told me that God had called me to lead and triple lead. I knew that was confirmation.

Being in the P.A.W. (Pentecostal Assemblies of the World) organization, the council held meetings four times annually. If you were called to ministry, you had to make it known at the meeting. When asked during the meeting if there were any new churches etc., I stepped out and told the board that God called me to pastor. My pastor who was surprised, was then asked about my character among other things. I had to have the Holy Ghost, be faithful in all things, have a good report, and no one could have spoken a railing accusation against me. Pastor answered adequately on my behalf. Upon completing all the requirements, I received my pastoral license there, and was later ordained by one of our district Elders in Lehigh Acres, Florida. Of course, I didn't tell my husband. The doctrine he was and is still under says woman are not allowed to preach or speak in public, or anywhere else for that matter. All I knew, was I had to see God for myself. This was over thirty years ago.

In 2001, I asked the Lord for a baby to have someone around the house when I got older. I didn't know it would work out just like that! As I said, Mother taught us radical faith... and I certainly BELIEVED! If you want a house, ask God, lay hands on that particular thing and by faith receive it. Give God His Word as He spoke it. God's Word must be coupled with faith. It works every time. Saints got houses that they were told they didn't qualify to get, new cars, healing in their body. Things just happened... and we knew it was all God.

Remember, I asked God for another baby. Before I learned I was pregnant, I was already buying baby things because I knew God would do just what He says. I told God that I wanted to have my baby before Christmas so that I could be up to fix my dinner. Then I thought... I can tell God just how I want it to happen. I said, "God, I want to have my baby on a

Wednesday so I can be home before the weekend, and I want it to be quick and easy."

One night as I was leaving church, a prayer warrior stopped my car and said, "I don't know what the devil is trying to do, but he is not going to do it. She laid her hands on my stomach and prayed for my unborn child. So, this would be my fifth child, my youngest was sixteen and I was forty-one.

One day, I went to the doctor and my perinatologist decided to keep me and induce labor. The doctor gave me Pitocin, which my body rejected. It caused my baby's heartbeat to drop dangerously low. The devil was telling me, my baby was going to die, but the Holy Ghost telling me to hold to the scriptures. So, I began to quote Proverbs 10:22, which says, "The blessing of the Lord, it maketh rich, and he addeth no sorrow with it." I said to God... "I asked You for this child, I didn't fornicate, I'm married." I continued to talk to God, and listened, while every heartbeat I heard sounded like it would be my baby's last.

The nurse removed the IV and immediately my baby's heartbeat kicked into a normal rhythm. Again, God did it! Before they took me down to perform surgery on me, they called my husband several times. He was too busy to stop whatever he was doing to come. After they could wait no longer, I was given a C-section. When my husband got there, the nurse was walking down the hall with our baby; it was all over. About a month or so later, the Lord spoke to me and said; 'You said you wanted it to be quick and easy.' I thought, 'Jesus thank you!!! That's why my body rejected the Pitocin. Pitocin is what brings on the labor pains.' God is so faithful!

Eventually, my husband and I purchased a real auto body and repair shop, that was fully equipped and bigger than the storefront we started out in. I worked in the office and turned a room into the nursery/lobby for us. We had all male employees. Business was pretty good. My husband did excellent work, and he didn't charge as much as other shops did.

Certain women would come to get their cars repaired and when I came outside the conversation would shift. I was no dummy. There was a particular woman among many, who was always there and forever in my face telling me about the latest Juanita Bynum CD. I knew she was up to no good because she was always at the shop. This lady had a reputation for being a loose woman that would get with married men.

Though she pretended to be in the ministry, she was a fake and people knew this about her. It was also well known that she had aids. However, that didn't stop her from flirting. I was not a jealous woman; my attitude was, money is money and there is no gender in money. Now, there were two guys that hung around the shop and helped for a fee of course! My older son, Ralph, was an adult, he would help his dad from time to time. Sometimes, they had disagreements because my husband didn't want to pay Ralph right. Ralph knew a lot about body work and he worked hard.

Ralph would see his dad flirting with women, but he would never tell me anything unless he got mad enough to say something. I could never figure out why my husband was never in a hurry to get home. He would leave the house about 7 a.m. and would get back home about 7- 8 p.m. I cooked dinner every day and would call him and beg him to come on home. He would say, "I'm coming, let me shoot this last coat of clear on the car, this is an insurance job, and I can't keep the car long." So, I would believe him. One thing about me, it never failed, every day around 4 p.m., I was at home with my children, cooking and looking forward to him coming home. This was my ritual. So, he knew he would be in the clear about that time. Finally, he would come home, take a bath, eat, and watch TV in the family room if I was in the bedroom. If I was in the family room, he would watch TV in the bedroom. There was a spirit about him that just could not take being around me very long. There was always a look in his eyes that I could see was an ungodly spirit within him. He said he had the Holy Spirit, but there were no signs that followed to give evidence. The spirit he had was not holy.

On the other hand, I played my gospel music which he could not stand. I often caught him listening to secular music when he was in the "Nobody's Right But Us" church. According to him, my pastor and our whole church was wrong because my pastor was a woman. Hmmm…

Let's go the Word

Philippians 4:3 says, "And I intreat thee also, true yokefellow, help those women which labored with me in the gospel, with Clement also, and *with* other my fellow laborers, whose names *are* in the book of life."

Reader, I am a witness that God's Word is true. Galatians 3:28 says, "There is neither Jew nor Greek, there is neither bond nor free, there is neither male nor female: for ye are all one in Christ Jesus." So many times, God has used me. Surely, if He can use a donkey, God can use a woman.

I recall one afternoon, I got a call from Miami. I thought my relative was laughing, but she was crying so hard, she could hardly talk. She asked me if I could go and see about her sister. I asked where she was. I turned around in the middle of the road to get to her! When I arrived at the lady's house, I went in with the intention to get her to the hospital immediately. Instead, I laid hands on her and began to pray for her. I totally forgot I was in someone else's house and that the lady had a daycare. When I came to myself, the lady and all the kids that could walk were peeping into the area where I was. I got her up and assisted her in getting into the truck. I called 911 and told them I was on the way to the hospital with a very sick person. I told them that I would be running red lights and stop signs. They asked me for the make and color of the vehicle. When we arrived at the hospital, they were waiting, and she was admitted.

Sometime later, this same relative that I took to the hospital came to visit me at my house. My husband bought up the subject about women preachers and how wrong they are. Immediately, she said, "Oh no, when I was sick and Guander prayed for me, I felt something drop in the bottom of my stomach." He could only be silent.

Normally, my husband took the baby to preschool, and

I really appreciated that. Later, I would go to the shop. Whenever I went and he was not there, it was hard to reach him on the phone. I would call him several times and sometimes I still didn't get him. I spent my days shopping, having lunch at the country club, or visiting the sick and shut in. I would run an errand if he asked me. There were always some people just hanging around gossiping. I did not approve of these people just hanging around. Of course, they looked better going than coming. They were glad to see me leave the shop so they could let it all hang out. There is something about wrong that will expose you. I had a suspicion that my husband was getting with other women. Like I said, I would wake up at night around 2-3 a.m. and he would be missing. I would call his cell and could not get him sometimes, or he would answer and tell me another lie. He would say, "Oh I had to come check on the shop." This went on for years!

As I said before, my husband was never fair with me when it came to money. He would dole out $80.00 to buy grocery for five people; then tell me he wanted to see the receipt. I would have to make up the difference and he knew it. I knew God would vindicate me. When it came to paying the light bill, the field guy knew him and when he had a disconnect order, he would come to the shop faithfully to collect the money so our lights at home would not be shut off. How crazy!!!! It's a fact, your bill must be paid once a month... so why not just pay it? That just really got on my nerves! But it didn't matter, he did it over and over. You see he handled the money. He would come home and have an envelope filled with hundreds and fifties. He kept his money in a coat pocket in the closet. I wasn't street savvy enough back then to see what was really going on.

There was a particular person that he claimed was his cousin, and I came across a cancelled check for $50.00 that he loaned or gave her. Remember, I only got $80.00 for groceries. I knew she wasn't a cousin. I knew his people. She was very disrespectful towards me and didn't even know me. Allow me to tell you, anytime a man or woman is disrespectful to you, it is because your spouse has been talking about you to that person. They have concluded they can disrespect you and get away with it. Well, this sister told me that the shop was public property, and she could come there whenever she wanted to. I told her that if she paid her way there, I would pay it back.

One evening my husband and I were standing in the back of the shop on MLK talking. This woman rolled up and walked through the shop like she owned it. She stood on the other side of my husband and started talking to him and totally ignoring me. The devil told her to grab his shoulder as if she was shaking something out of her shoe. When she did, before I realized it or even knew it, I had jumped on her. There we were fighting on the sidewalk at the shop. My husband kept telling ME to stop! This man drew back his fist and hit me as hard as he could! Can you believe this! He did this two or three times in order to get me off of her. When she was able to get up, she got in her car and left. Soon after, I left the shop also to keep from doing something I would regret later.

I immediately went to my Associate Pastor and told her what happened, and that I was going to sit myself down from church duties. She told me right then and there, "No you are not! She provoked you." She asked me if whipped her good? Then told me that I was restored and that she had no business doing what she did. I went home thinking how tired I was of that madness and when and how would it ever end? I thought to myself, 'I'm here, I've been here all my life, family, church, everything's here. I began to wonder will this happen for the rest of my life. My husband's pastor told him to get his clothes and leave, which he did. I was so tired of the madness! When, if at all, will it ever stop? He eventually came back home. I forgave him because I had to. I didn't tell my son's because it would have gotten ugly. I was depending on God to do what He said He would do.

Romans 12:19 says, "Dearly beloved, avenge not yourselves, but *rather* give place unto wrath: for it is written, Vengeance *is* mine; I will repay, saith the Lord."

Chapter 6

Transition

The year is 2008 and my dining room has been packed up in boxes for over a year as if I had somewhere to go. The boxes in the corner have dust on them. I'm sure my neighbor is laughing at me and saying that I have been saying for longest time that I'm moving.

I know faith is an action word and little did she know, I was moving in the natural and the spiritual. I thought if I remodeled the house, it would make me want to stay. So, we added 1,200 more square feet to the house. I added a room across the entire back of the house. I also added French doors, half circle windows, a cathedral ceiling with shelves, and a bathroom in the bedroom. The new bathroom was very spacious; it had wood cabinets, gold faucets, a cathedral ceiling, and a huge shower. Even after all of that, I still could not bring myself to be content. God had a plan.

There was a new community being built, Ryland Homes, and I wanted so badly to buy a house there. We met with a salesman for the new subdivision. The house I wanted was huge, with a swimming pool. The salesman said our down payment would be $22,000. My husband gave me a check for the down payment, but overnight he changed his mind. I'm sure you can guess who had to face the people to get the check back. That's right, me! He said the mortgage payment would be around $2000 a month. So, I looked at smaller houses, but in the same subdivision because that is where I really wanted to be.

Soon after, my husband's cousins were moving to north Georgia. They had a nice place, whether they were leasing or buying. They stressed the fact that the homes were big and what you paid $200,000 for in Georgia, you would pay around $600,000 in Florida. He had relatives that had lived in North Georgia for many years. At the time my husband's relatives were moving from Florida to several different cities and states. My husband has always been a follower. So, it wasn't surprising that he was considering moving to Georgia when his relatives decided they were moving. Plus, he had gone on a trip to North

Georgia, which also made him lean toward moving to Georgia. Or did it?

He came home and asked if I would like to move to the Atlanta area. He was so hyped up! After he convinced me that he was serious, I told him, "Of course, I would like to move." I was thinking, 'he doesn't know people there so, I will at least have more time with him when he gets off work.' So, I spent nights, sometimes all night, online looking at houses. Whenever I came across a house that I liked and it was within my budget, I called the realtor. I made two trips to North Georgia looking at homes. The sad part is it was just me; my husband would not take the time to go help me look for a house. Once my son that was in college in Tampa went with me to look at some homes in Georgia.

Finally, I saw a beautiful four-sided brick home, with five bedrooms, three baths, two car garages, and a large yard in a cul-de-sac. This was the one! I called my realtor; the bank accepted my bid, and the closing date was set for the following Friday. My husband didn't go with me to the closing. Instead, I went alone with two big cashier checks to pay for the house. That morning, the temperature in Stockbridge, Georgia was only 17 degrees. The realtor met me downstairs at the hotel where I was staying, and we proceeded to the closing.

Once there, I exchanged the money for the deeds to the house. Then I told the person that I wanted to put my husband's name on the deed also. She told me in the state of Georgia the person must be present to have their name added. At the time, I did not realize that God had gone before me to make what would have been a crooked path, straight! Later that day, my husband arrived with the boys. We looked the house over and were very pleased. The house was only five years old. I do not remember if we stayed there that night. I already had the utilities turned on, so the next day we cleaned the house. Later, we got it painted and bought a few appliances.

Shortly after, we returned to Florida, traveling in two separate vehicles. Prior to leaving I told the president of the HOA that I would be back in a month. I recruited help to assist me with packing the rest of the items. By faith I had already purchased furniture in Florida. The month passed before I knew it. My uncle in Miami worked for a moving company. He and a helper came to move me to Georgia. I rented the biggest truck U-Haul had and the next size. The movers arrived that evening and worked until early in the morning, while my husband sat down and watched them. He did not lift a pencil; he had a strategy in place. He asked me if he helped the movers pack, would I allow the baby to go to the church that he attended? He already knew the answer was, no. Then he said, "Well, I'm not helping you pack!" He sat there watching television until it was time to break the cabinet down and load the television on the truck. All this was a front, so he didn't have to help at all. The movers worked over into the night, they had to get some rest. I was thinking we would leave early the next morning, but I had so much to be loaded, it was the following night before they were finished loading.

Finally, it was just about time to head to Georgia. However, my husband did not plan, want, or ever intend to accompany us to Georgia. He said he could not just up and leave his business, he had to work. He didn't even plan to go help us move in or unpack the furniture. Nevertheless, the time was at hand for me to make my exodus. The two trucks were loaded, my vehicle was packed with my personal things, it was go time! I was sad to leave my husband and family, but happy at the same time. As I pulled away in my black, '06 Chrysler 300, I was singing, "We are moving on up!"

How strange is it for a husband not to accompany his family to a new city and state, a place of total strangers, or not to even help them get the house set up? Somehow, it never fazed my husband. As we all heard for over thirty years... he had a car to finish. How low can you go? Our youngest son was six years old at the time, and it didn't bother his dad in the least to see him go. Praise God, my two adult sons traveled with us to help us unload when we reached our destination. Finally, around 4 a.m. we arrived at our new home.

Please allow me to inject this... Funny thing, about a year earlier, as I was unlocking the front door of our house in Florida, my baby boy looked up at me and said, "This is not our house, we have another house; we are just staying here until the people come." Then he walked in the house as if he had not said anything. Another time a relative passed and we were at the house of the deceased. My baby was walking up and down the stairs; when he told his dad that there was a man in the room upstairs who told him not to run so he wouldn't hurt himself. They were spooked because that was the room where the deceased slept and there was no one upstairs! My baby said he could not see the man's face because the television light was shining. This weirded them all out, they asked if my son was special. I have come to realize he is special.

Now getting back to our arrival to our new home. Well, we were all tired, so we got food from the Waffle House, and everyone took a short nap. The next morning, my grown boys were up early unpacking so they could go back to Florida. Once the furniture was in place, it was the moment of truth. Everyone was about to leave me and my two younger sons all alone in a new town and state that we had never been to or heard of. My heart sank, I wanted my husband, mama, sister anybody from Florida! I didn't know anyone but Jesus in that city. Suddenly, I changed my mind because I was scared. As they pulled away, I felt like running behind the vehicle and yelling, wait I changed my mind. I was in too deep, but I had to be strong for my children. Praise God for a GPS! I didn't know what stores were there, where they were, or how to get to them. So, I used the GPS for everything. I felt so alone, as if I was on the planet alone.

Soon after, my son that was in Tampa, Florida going to college, decided to move to Georgia. The new house was so big, it took some time getting used to that much space. The entryway was the size of a bedroom. The master suite was about 800 square feet, with a nursery in the room. I was afraid to sleep in that master bedroom for three months. To enter the master suite, you came through double doors, then down a hallway before you could be seen. My baby slept with me until he was twelve years old. I was not used to a huge split-level house. I was accustomed to having my husband and sons in the house; it was all new to me.

About two weeks later, my son left Tampa and moved to North Georgia. He was hired on the spot at a fortune five hundred company (that was God's favor). Because his new position, we were able to fly non-revenue to anywhere in the world. Still, in the span of three plus years, my husband came to visit us about twelve or thirteen times. All he had to do was show up and board the plane; it didn't cost him a prayer. I remember, one Easter my youngest was looking forward to spending time with his dad. My husband called and said he missed the plane. How? Flights left every other hour going to Atlanta, Georgia. He just had other plans with other folks. My baby cried and cried. He told his dad he was supposed to be with us. I was disappointed as well; I was so used to cooking a big dinner and watching my husband enjoy it.

Sometimes, I flew to Florida to be with my husband. The house would be so dusty, I could hardly breathe. He made sure that he had bottled water and sodas in the house; we would go out to eat. He never spent a whole day with me; he would never take a day off. I only got whatever time he had left after working. The house was pretty much empty. I only left a few things there to keep him comfortable, because the plan was for him to move to Georgia a few months after me and the kids. Here it had been over a year, and he wasn't even talking about joining us. When I would mention it, he would get upset. Whenever he decided to visit, he caught the last plane to Atlanta and the first one going back to Florida. Once he stayed six days with us, other than that, he came late Friday and left Sunday. This was his norm.

So now it is 2012, it has been three years and still no husband. He was singing the same ole song about work. One time, I went to visit him in Florida, rented a brand new, black Dodge Charger. It was my custom with all rentals to put the rental agreement in the glove compartment, which I did. As usual, that day we went out to eat, etc. At the house, the breakfast nook in the dining room was filled with mail. The left and right counters in the kitchen and the stove top were also covered with mail. I was beginning to be concerned.

The next morning, I got up and went to see a friend. As we walked towards my rental car she said, "You have gum along the side of your car." I could see the long white line. As we got closer to the car, we realized it was scratched down to the metal on both sides, and on the back! I could not imagine what happened, the drug boys in the neighborhood always looked out for me. I asked my husband if he drove the car, he said no. Of course, he tried to make me believe that I scratched the car on the chain link fence when I went to visit a church mother. How could that be? He was very upset with me and declared he didn't do it. I told him, "Well you need to fix it." We owned an auto body and repair shop, so he found some left over black paint and shot some on the scratch to cover it. I don't think he sanded it or filled it with bondo.

For the life of me, I could not imagine what happened to the car. I prayed and asked God for what seemed like a long time. This is what happened… He didn't drive the car, but while I was sleeping, he went through my purse, through my phone, read text messages, and went in the car took the rental agreement and torn it up. Then he viciously dug into the side of the car with a screwdriver or some hard metal object. God cannot lie!

Three plus years later, he still had not come to be with his family. He gave the same ole excuses. One night, I was lying in my bed and the Holy Ghost spoke to me and said, 'He is going with Debra.' I said, "What!" I called him immediately and asked him if he was going with this woman. He said, "Guander, what are you talking about?" "The Holy Ghost doesn't lie," I told him. Knowing me like he did, he admitted to it. I told him, "I tell you what, y'all can have each other!" This woman attended the same movement as him. She was a known lesbian and had been for over thirty years. She wore men's clothes, sagging jeans with boxers showing. I was somewhat hurt to say the least. Of all the females, why her? I called my son immediately and told him to get me a ticket to Florida. I wasted no time in filing for my divorce.

As the saying goes, you're always the last to find out... Well, many people knew what was going on. They just never said anything to me, until I said something. However, I did find out why he always left the house so early in the mornings. He was meeting a woman that drove the school bus in between her bus routes for years. I went to her house, but she was not home. So, I made a second trip. From outside, I could hear her talking loudly. When I touched the hood of her car, it was still hot. This let me know that she had just gotten home. Would you believe my husband called the woman and told her that I was coming over there! That's who she was talking so loudly to on the phone.

When I rung her doorbell, there was complete silence. I was wrong for going to her house. The man was married to me; this woman could only do as much as he allowed her to. She was just one of many. How could a man be so callous to convince his wife and family to move to another state with the promise of joining them, but totally deceive them by never joining them? I spent 37 years of my life with this man and did not know him! Y'all, I really didn't know him.

When he found out I was seeking a divorce, the real him was revealed. I was told he was using drugs, which explains the time he came to visit and was in a glassy eyed, mental straight jacket. He couldn't respond to me. He just sat there staring at the wall instead of the television. I was told that state is known as being stuck.

Now, this man set out to assassinate my character, which he could not because your works speak for you. Nevertheless, he went from house to house telling lies, dubious lies! In court, he told the judge the same delusional lies. It was very sad. He also went to every person that he knew I talked to and told them lies. He even went to my aunt and told her that he was not marrying me again! My thought was, can I get that in writing! How delusional could he be? He talked about me to people that didn't even know me. He told my son that I was going to lose my mind and walk the streets in sandals. I guess that was his intention for me when he stole my dress and skirt suit and took it to a witch. Guess what, no weapon formed against me shall prosper.

I recall onetime, when he was in Atlanta that he tried to burst the window of my car with me and the kids in the car. My youngest son called 911! The lies continued. People were calling me left and right talking about how unhinged he was.

There were neigh-sayers in his ear telling him what they would do if they were him. The sad part is he listened and did what they said. The bailiff said my husband's attorney charged $600 an hour. I knew his attorney was a demon on assignment. How could anyone take advantage of a person's feeble mind?

Now that everything was coming out, my relatives began to speak on things they witnessed. The greatest thing about anything is the real will all ways be revealed! A person that I always thought to be close to me, told me she knew how he was saying he was not going to Atlanta. I asked her why she didn't tell me, that's people for you. Understand, I would not have left Florida to move to Georgia for a million dollars! Of all the lies and scandals, I never once struck back. See God will never help you fight; He will fight for you! Because of how I knew God, I knew whatever He did, He only had to do it once. God does all things well. (Mark 7:37)

It was difficult for me to take care of my legal affairs and deal with all that I was facing. I did not have the finances to hire an attorney for his circus. Again, I was in a new town without anyone to help me. I cried so many tears, not because of his infidelity, but because I felt sorry for my kids. I felt sorry for myself. I had no one, I do mean no one! People will only go so far with you and get tired quickly. My God had a ram in the bush for me and he was not caught in the thicket. Bless God! I thank God for the hearts of those that He touched to meet me and my family's needs during that time.

Finally, the day came for our mediation. I gave my husband the home in Florida, the business, money, cars, and commercial property. I walked away with the home in Georgia and a '06 Chrysler. I didn't ask for spousal support. I just wanted out! Because he had his thing going on he gave me less than $300 for child support. As late as 2018, he still refused to do right by his child.

No matter what, I stood on the Word of God, which taught me in Joel 2:25 that I would recover the years that the locust, cankerworm, caterpillar, and the palmerworm has eaten. God cannot lie. The battle was not mine; it was the Lord's. My son told me I was crazy, and about things his dad had done. He felt like I was just letting his dad walk all over me. I told him, "No, I'm a woman of God and I must always have an excellent spirit." People say if you dig one ditch, you better dig two; and we understand what they mean by this; but that is not scripture. In Proverbs 26:27 God says, "Whoso diggeth a pit shall fall therein: and he that rolleth a stone, it will return upon him."

For the 37 years that me and my husband were together, his family was always okay with me. That changed once we divorced. How many people know that people will turn against you for no reason? That alone spoke volumes, because it let me know that they were not real from the beginning. I have to say of his family there is only one person that still treats me the same. I have learned, it doesn't matter what you are going through or may go through, you can make it by the grace of God.

I recall this lady who belonged to the same movement as my ex-husband. She came to the shop nearly every day to borrow money to buy pills. If it is a lie, the Ex told it. I thought she was on crack; he said no, it was pills. How crazy! As if that is something to write home about, pills weren't any better. Since I moved to Georgia, I was told she passed. The way a tree falls, is the way it lies.

I was still learning more about my Ex... During a trip to Florida in 2017, I was told my godmother, whose life I was in since high school, a woman I looked up to and had much respect for had taken part in helping my then husband deceive me. Her family members knew me and had since the 70's. This so-called Christian woman knew my husband was going with her sister. She allowed them to lay up at her house. When they came to Florida, they would meet him at their cousin's house. My husband would bring money to her sister for the hotel they would lay up in.

Another time, during a trip to Florida for one of my court dates, I stopped by to visit an elderly relative. One of her friends stopped by and as we were introduced, she casually said to me "Dot and her sister sat in my yard fanning mosquitoes a many nights, waiting on your husband to bring money. Where did that come from? God will make the devil talk. Now my thing was this, if you knew that and didn't tell, you were just as guilty!

I don't have to tell you, the sister that was going with my then husband is dead and has been for close to 10 years. She broke her neck and went from nursing home to nursing home. I'm sure he sent money when she died. God does not slumber, nor does He forget. I do not wish any ill will on my enemy. However, your deeds will slow walk you down. God said, 'Whosoever breaks a hedge a serpent shall bite him.' (Ecclesiastes 10:8)

All I had was God and His Word and that was more than enough. I cannot find the words to tell you the pain I have endured. All the time the man was looking me in the face and telling me lies, like it was all good. That's why the matter fell the way it did. It would be so easy for me to carry more baggage than Delta and allow the scars of my past to dictate my future. The devil is a liar and his grandma too! Before I take it back, I'll add more to it!

Understand, the husband God has for me didn't do those hurtful things to me. The one I choice to marry, getting ahead of God, is who hurt me. I will not cut off my nose to spite my face. Never allow any man or woman to have that kind of power over you. Never rob yourself.

Let's go to the Word in Isaiah 43:13, which says, "Yea, before the day was I am He; and there is none that can deliver out of my hand: I will work, and who shall let it?

Simply put, this scripture is saying, who can tell God what to do, who can do better than what God has preordained; no one can alter the plans of God, no not one.

Chapter 7
Court

So, I've been divorced for a while now. Today, I received a summon to appear in court. The summons was sent via US postal mail and email. I consented to giving my husband eighty percent of the marital assets. All I wanted was out. I couldn't imagine why I was receiving a summons from the Florida court. The divorce was over, dead, benediction spoken, the repass over and had been for some time! So, why? Well, the summon was for some frivolous accusations. I was accused of not taking care of my sons, not paying my bills, and my lights always being off. I knew it was only backlash and retaliation from my ex-husband. I will say this, the truth needs no defense.

My trips to Florida were a hard push. I'm so grateful for my son Marlon. He saw to it that I had money and many times a hotel. I wasn't broke but bent a lot of times. There were times when I didn't go to sleep at night because I had to be up at 2 a.m. to drive to Jackson, Georgia to drop my sons off at Mother Daisy's house. She was a wonderful saint that blessed me and my sons tremendously. I would then head to Hartsfield Airport to make the 6 a.m. flight to Florida to be at my 9 a.m. appointment in court. When I went to court in response to summons regarding my children, I was told that I had to appear in court with my son on the next court date. At the next appearance, my son was taken to a private area where a court appointed attorney spoke with him. After which, the allegations were immediately dismissed.

Now back home in Georgia, one day as I was driving, I noticed this church, Community United Pentecostal Church (UPC). Just looking at the church, somehow, I knew that was the place I wanted to be. Mind you, I'm not one to go any and everywhere called church, because people now are preaching another Jesus. As carefully thought out through prayer, I visited UPC. As a lady and her sons were about to go into church, I asked her has church started. She replied, "Yes, but come on in, sit by me," she was so kind. After service she gave me her name and phone number. A few days later, I was in Florida and my son needed help with his car in Georgia. Remember, before I didn't know anyone in the city. Now, I'd met this very kind lady at church, Sister Willie Ruth Farley Akins. She and her husband, Deacon Jimmy Akins drove about 40 minutes one way to help my son. I will never forget it. To this very day, she is one of my best friends. Allow me to say, in a lifetime if you have five true friends, you have done well. Evangelist Willie Ruth Farely Akins is a friend in word and deed.

The saints at UPC were so kind. To name a few, Evangelist Kiera Evans, and Evangelist Raquel Evans Williams. The church was wonderful. The pastor, Bishop Herman Barber, was one of the kindest, and most humble men of God you'd ever want to meet. However, though kind, he was no nonsense. I love the way the church service was carried out. Community UPC on Old Griffin Road took me back to a place in God that I hadn't been in years. Mother Mildred Barber, the pastor's wife, was a holy and righteous mother in Zion. I saw something in Bishop Herman Barber that made me think of Eli and Samuel. After one service, I took my son, Yanni, to Bishop Barber and asked him to bless my son. Bishop Barber looked at me and so kindly laid hands on him and blessed him. (Acts 8:17) Praise God for fellowship with those that are sanctified.

I received another summons from Florida. This time it was for a paternity test. The document stated my husband was informed by a friend of the family that when my youngest child was conceived, I was having an affair. Wow! So, I was sent to this dirty lab to have my son tested. I was not happy. I knew this man was being coached by some evil person, or was he the person? The test was completed, and the results were 99.9995 positive.

I felt so sad, but especially for my son. My baby could not understand why he was on this roller coaster ride. He cried when his dad didn't come visit him one Easter, now this. The man was only paying $300 dollars a month for child support, but no medical, vision, or dental coverage was given to his child. Nothing! It all came from my pocket. To this very day he still owes me back child support.

Yet another summon was received for court in Florida. Every trip I made costed me money. My son told me his dad said I was going to lose my mind and walk the streets in flip flops. That's exactly what he was trying to do, break me mentally. It was a common occurrence for me not to get adequate rest just to be on time for court. When I arrived at the courthouse... would you know there was a continuation. Meaning court was cancelled and no one told me. Allow me to be clear, court was so often that my son could not attend a traditional school. He had to do home school so that he could work from anywhere and believe me, my 10-year-old did just that. He did his lesson from the back seat of my car while traveling on I-75, or at a hotel computer, which can be quite disturbing for a child.

For a very small span of time, my youngest was able to attend a traditional school. One day during this time, I stopped at the Salvation Army, which wasn't far from the school. While there I received a call from a school official asking me to come pick up my son. When I arrived, there had been a situation. My son was in the lunchroom getting his lunch, when he looked over and saw his dad sitting at one of the tables. This man traveled over 600 miles to traumatize my son in the name of having lunch together. Yanni left his tray, ran to the office in fear and locked himself in a closet. People were trying to figure out what was going on. Yanni had friends that backed him. They went to the office to see if Yanni was alright. The principle told them to leave, but they refused to until they knew what was going on. The guidance counselor went to the closet door in tears and said, "It's me open the door." She was the only person he would open the door for.

I think they told his dad to leave. Lord knows, God was keeping me, because they attempted to call me several times, but my phone did not ring. His dad was gone upon my arrival, but the kids were still stirred up. I felt so sad for my child. He was afraid of his dad and wanted nothing to do with him. I told the school the only other person that could see my son at school was his brother; that other than me and him NO one else was allowed. Please help me make sense of a man wanting to eat lunch with a child he previously said was not his.

So, now I wasn't getting a summons to appear before the judge for one thing anymore! I was receiving orders on motions for several different accusations at once. This was just the tip of the iceberg. The summons had become a common occurrence, so my attitude was, what's next. As I stated earlier, the summons came via US mail and email. One day, while on my way to Kroger, my phone alerted me that I had a text. I peeped at the text while driving; it was a summons for court. As I read the word summon, I somehow began to see myself slowly falling to the right side onto the passenger seat. It was as if I was suddenly outside of my body and watching from an elevated place. Before I completely fell to the passenger's side, I heard a voice say... 'THE LORD IS MY LIGHT AND MY SALVATION, WHOM SHALL I FEAR, which is Psalm 27:1. Immediately upon hearing the Word of God, I was snatched back into an upright position. It seemed it all happened in a matter of seconds. I know it was the Hand of God. This is what I call a demonic court hydra because I went to court every month, and sometimes twice a month, for about two years. Please remember, during this time we were divorced and had been for some time; so clearly, this was backlash and retaliation.

Not long after, I got a call informing me that my dad was very ill and I needed to come to Thomasville, Georgia. In between court dates, I was able to go, but I just didn't have the funds to move like I wanted. Nevertheless, I still went. Sugar, my sister from New York was there and she was a blessing to me. She paid for my children's meals. Bless God. After a few days, I was about to head home to North Georgia. Wait, let me stop right here and say God, The Most High will make you tell what you were supposed to keep secret! My stepbrother says to me, "I guess they didn't get all the cancer out." I could have screamed, what the world! Then he said, "If I were you, I would stay a few more days."

I was shocked that my dad had cancer all that time and his wife gathered her children and told them, but hid it from me, my daddy's baby. She was wrong for that. The Lord was leading me to go home, but I didn't listen. I stayed another day.

On the way home, a sleep came over me that I can't explain. Even over the counter stimulates did not help.

In a few days, I received a call informing me that my dad had passed. It hurt me that he died knowing I was going through so much madness. I had less than $90 dollars to travel with, and I had to get a hotel room, food, gas, etc. Still, I made hotel reservations and packed our clothes. Not knowing how or where, I moved just like Father Abraham and left with a full tank of gas and maybe $80 dollars.

The Word of God says as the lepers went, they were healed (St. Luke 17:14). Let me tell you, as I drove down I-75, I was getting calls from people that were sending me money. My cousin, Bishop Larry M. Rayner and his lovely wife, Mother Mamie Rayner of Junior Church of Christ Holiness, paid for my lodging. God will always do what He says. My older sons came from Florida to attend their granddad's homegoing. I just could not figure out why their dad came. Though it was not a good occasion, it was good to have all my sons together.

Now back at home, I received another summon. My Ex was petitioning the court for joint visitation. After the hearing of the case, the judge granted him visitations. However, the judge said if he didn't want to go with his dad, he didn't have to. Later that day, I picked up my son and told him what happened in court. He had me call his dad so that he could tell him he didn't want to go with him. His dad was saying, "But I'm your daddy." Yanni said, "I told you, I don't want to go with you; I don't want to go!" So that was the end of that.

I'm not sure exactly when, but I recall my friend from the movie "The Apostle" for reasons unknown to me at the time, insisted that I introduce myself to one of our city officials. To me, it was nonsense. Why would I do that, what was I going to say? I didn't tell him, but I just knew I wasn't going to do what he kept suggesting. Then one morning as I was driving, I had an unction to do what Prophet Carl had told me to do all along. When I obeyed, it was unbelievable how things began to shift.

I recall another time when I was taking my son to school, I ran out of gas, and I had no money. I knew that the police official's duty was to protect and serve. So, I decided to call the department to have them bring me gas. I told the woman who answered my call what I needed. She said she could call her neighbor to help, which she did. He came with gas and didn't charge anything.

On another occasion, I was not feeling well at all, was riding on red, and I had maybe $4 dollars. The doctor had given me a prescription and I was on the way to the pharmacy, when I thought... Wait a minute, I don't have the money to buy gas and my medication. I had to do one or the other. The Holy Ghost told me to call Chubby, she's my aunt Marilyn Howard in Miami, Florida. She has always been a kindhearted person. Without hesitation, she sent money, and I did what I needed to.

I cried so many tears for so many nights. Not because of my ex-husband, but because I knew I lived righteous, yet here I am in a strange land not knowing how to get to point A to B without a Garman. Oh, but I had to be strong for my children; I never allowed them to see me cry.

I was thinking one day about my overall situation, and something occurred to me. When I lived in Florida, I found a piece of paper with directions to Baxley, Georgia. They were the exact directions Ann had given me, verbatim. So, I knew she had to have given them to him. One day, my son asked me who was Val. I told him Val was Ann's sister. That let me know she had been calling my husband. When God pulled off the cover, it was revealed that Ann had been cloaking for her sister and my husband for years. Ann always told me that I lived better than a family with two people working. I brushed it off and thought nothing of it.

Let me tell you, Ann was singing in the choir, and she was close to me. I shared a lot of things with her. This woman had been in my life since high school. THAT IS HOW A SNAKE CAN STRIKE, BY ALLOWING IT TO BE IN YOUR BOSOM. Never allow people to get up on you. Everybody is sent by God or Satan. This woman and her sister were spending my husband's money and had been for years. They were not the only women. There were others locally that laughed in my face and endeavored to take my place. The back story with Ann and her sister is that they both are dead now.

It had been some time since I last received anything, now I had another summon in the mail. Honestly, I lost track. I think of the times that I went to Florida for court and how I had to sleep at my sister's house many times. Random friends picked me up and dropped me off. Having to leave my children in another state with someone to answer to was just unbelievable and utterly nonsense. I'd been through Hartsfield Jackson Airport so often, they knew me. I thought of my ex-husband and his high price attorney strutting down the corridors of the courthouse, while I walked alone with not even enough money for a sit-down meal. His attorney would speak to me with a smirk on his face. How many people know I was not alone. Jesus was there all the time working. I couldn't see him and most of the time I couldn't feel him, but I know He was with me.

When I went to court, I was instructed by an official to park in a certain spot that was created just for me, not an official parking space. I went through security and arrived at the assigned court room. When our names were called, we approached the tables. I spoke first and after I finished speaking, the judge responded to me and walked into his chamber. As I attempted to stand up, I was yanked down, then I heard a voice say, "Wait." It was an officer. I had no idea what was going on. The officer talking through an earpiece said, "Is he still in the bathroom?" Then it occurred to me, I had security in and out of the court room. The officer that yanked me back into my seat was communicating with another officer stationed outside. I was offered an escort as well. I just believe I know how Elijah felt on Mount Carmel. When I obeyed the man of God, things shifted. (You can read about Elijah at Mount Carmel in 1 Kings 18:2 – 46.)

Of all the things, my husband took my grey and blue dress to a witch to put witchcraft on me, as well as other items of mine. The Word of God warns us not to be ignorant of Satan's devices. God is real and so is Satan. Too often we want to hear about Shadrach, Meshach, and Abednego and all of that is good. However, we need to know about the playbook of Satan. I'm a believer in St. Mark 16:17-18 that says, "And these signs shall follow them that believe; In my name shall they cast out devils; they shall speak with new tongues; They shall take up serpents; and if they drink any deadly thing, it shall not hurt them; they shall lay hands on the sick, and they shall recover.

You do know Satan was once in heaven, at the time his name was Lucifer. War broke out in heaven and he and his angels were cast out by Archangel Michael. (Revelations 12:7-9 God changed his name to Satan and he has been mad ever since he hit the ground. Understand he hates all of God's creation. His mission is to steal, kill and destroy. He is a master deceiver. Our fight is never with flesh and blood, but it is spiritual. (Ephesians 6:12 It was not my husband; it was Satan using him. Unknowingly, we are often angry with the wrong source. It's not the person but the devil working through them, because at some point in time a door was opened.

Reader, all good comes from the Most High God. (James 1:17 Don't think of yourself more highly than you should. It was God and His infinite mercy. It could have been me or you used by Satan. I pray that God will constantly create in me a clean heart. I don't hate my ex-husband. Yet, I don't fellowship with him in any shape or form.

So, here we were back in court before the same judge. He told my ex-husband, "You asked for joint visitations and I granted it; there is nothing more I can do for you." He told him that he needed to find another court room to play in. Returning from court, as I unlocked and opened the door and got about three steps or so into the house, I heard God say... JUST AS I WAS WITH MOSES SO SHALL I BE WITH YOU. I thanked and praised the Lord. God was doing just that.

Chapter 8

All To Him I Owe

"Come on, let's go to the flea market." I reminded this sister that it was cold outside, and I didn't want to go out. She would not give up. Eventually, I gave in, even though I did not want to pack up the items and drive to the flea market knowing that we might not sell anything.

When we arrived, we set up tables across from each other. It was cold, so I sat in the car most of the time until I had a customer. The customers came randomly. Some just looking, while others purchased items. One of the customers was a gentleman inquiring about a clock. I could tell he was a Christian. He wanted to know if I would take a dollar less for the clock and I agreed. He smiled and stated he had to get on a conference call but assured me he would be back to purchase the clock. I was thinking to myself, why does he continue to tell me that he's coming back. If he does that will be fine and if he doesn't that will be fine too. The sister said, "Umm, that might be your husband." I told her, "Girl you know that man is probably married."

In an hour or so, the gentleman came back. He said, "I told you I was coming back." I'm not sure how we started talking, but we chatted for about an hour, mainly talking about the Lord. Finally, I said, "Well okay, I'm going to let you go. I don't want your wife to think the wrong thing." That was my way of slick finding out if he was married. That man looked at me as if I had cussed his great grandma. He said, "If I was married, do you think I would be standing here this long talking to you?" I don't remember what I said. He asked for my number and gave me his. To this day, I have the paper he wrote his phone number on. Then he asked if he could have a picture of me. Normally, bells and whistles would have gone off in my head, but for some reason, I was okay with it. He told me he was a Sunday school teacher and the name of the church he attended. I may have told him that we would visit.

A good bit of time had passed and Yanni was doing well in school. It turned out to be a good thing that he did home school. What the devil meant for bad, God turned it around. He really loved church. I cannot explain it, but he played drums, keyboard, organ, and bass guitar. Would you believe he has never had a lesson or been coached? He was about four years old when he asked for a drum set. We bought it from Toys R Us. Years later, he just up and started playing the keyboard that I purchased for me to learn how to play. One day he asked for a bass guitar. So, off to the music store we went. I bought him a bass guitar and an amplifier. He loved to play at our church, Community UPC, and at any of our sister churches. I just wanted him to bless God and play to the Glory of God.

I thank God for every church He is magnified in. I must say, Community UPC declared Holiness unto the Lord. If you were looking for a church with a thousand people, then it was not the church for you. If you wanted to be saved, sanctified, and filled with the Holy Ghost, you were at the right place! Over the years, I watched the saints be consistent and that continues to this day. Some of them, the Lord has called to their reward. Holiness is still right! This is what Mother Mildred Barber, and the saints stood on.

Yanni was the first to let me know that he wanted Community UPC to be his church home, then his brother. I was the last, but not the least to become a member. You see, I was already a licensed and ordained pastor, evangelist, and teacher. However, although I had the life and credentials, I was yet out of order. God had to reveal to me that every leader needs a pastor. God doesn't have any lone rangers. My former pastor in Florida was deceased. I stand to tell you that after becoming a member of Community UPC, I felt that old feeling that I recognized in the Lord. Of course, when I marry a preacher, prophet, or whomever the Lord has for me, I will be with him in total oneness. God just doesn't bless out of order. The head of the woman is the man.

Though I lived in Georgia, I always kept in touch with my family in Florida. I got the news that my mom was not doing the best. We traveled to Florida to visit her. I must brag on my siblings. I really don't think it was possible for anyone to get better care than she received. When my mom's health began to decline, she was admitted to a five-star assisted living facility. Family, children, and friends always had her on the go. She really enjoyed herself and didn't miss services at her own church. I'm so grateful that my siblings were on one accord and gave our mom the best care.

Though I didn't have the money to help, none of my siblings ever made me feel any type of way. They all treated me as if I was contributing. My younger sister is a Registered Nurse, and she has a Master of Social Work degree. She was an in-house blessing. Look how God places who you need, where and when they are needed. God works strategically.

This is exactly how God moved with Van, the Christian man I met at the flea market. We talked from time to time. He was very humble and modest. Yes, he taught Sunday school, and he was the pastor. Over the years, I've known him to be an honorable man that loves his family and church. This man of God has been an asset to my life. God just worked as only God can; by having the right person in the right place, at the right time.

Despite, all the situations I've been through, God always showed himself strong. Like when I went to a hospital in Atlanta, Georgia, for surgery. A rule I always honor is to never go to any hospital for treatment alone. My sister and her husband went with me for my surgery. While waiting on my doctor, the anesthesiologist and I had some words. I am convinced that he purposely gave me a massive amount of medication. My sister said I didn't wake up until it was almost night. She said it took over six hours for me to wake up. I am convinced this man tried to kill me with a lethal overdose.

After so much time had passed and I still was not awake, she called my other sister in Florida crying. She told her I could not wake up. My sister and her husband, Elder Jerry Clarke, a powerful man of God and pastor of Lighthouse Church, prayed me through. The devil tried to kill me, but as my pastor, Mother Mildred Barber would say, "God is the devil's boss." Reader, I need you to understand, people are people first, and they are their profession second. For example... As a person, a medical professional may share things with someone they trust that HIPPA would fine them for sharing.

God tells us not to put our trust in the arm of flesh. (Jeremiah 17:5) God promised that we all must stand before the judgement seat of Christ; that everyone will receive the things done in their body, whether good or bad. This is why I didn't retaliate against my husband. As I mentioned, my son told me I was crazy to allow his dad to do the things he did. I understood when you do certain things, you open gates, doors, and portals to demonic forces. That alone is torment. Remember the man of Gadarene in St. Mark 5:1-20.

As I've said and cannot say enough, God will fight for you. I can say my trials became my testimony and better days were here! God blessed my youngest son Yanni to graduate in spite of the circumstances we went through. My soul loves Jesus! It was nobody but God that kept me and loved me

enough to lead and guide me into all truth. There were times when death was all around us, oh but God!

As I mentioned, going to Saint Petersburg, I was a bit nervous and debating whether to drive across the Sky Way Bridge. At the time, the highest point if I'm not mistaken was 9 miles high. God said to me, you have done things more dangerous than this. I have found God to be what you need Him to be; there are so many facets of God. The way I see it, God allows things to happen because like with Jesus, there is a *must need to go through Samaria.* This is where the woman met Jesus at the well in Samaria as He was on His way to Galilee. Remember, Samaria was the detour that God placed on Jesus's journey. God places necessary detours on our journey as well. I often say, "What you go through is contingent upon your calling." I'm grateful, God has done what He said He would do. His Word cannot fall to the ground. He watches over His Word to perform it.

I can remember, how I was shy and ashamed to really praise God and dance before the Lord in church. During the time, I was a member of House of Prayer and there was a sister from the church, whose testimony changed my life! She was legally blind and though traveling with the assistance of the flight attendants, she was boarded onto the wrong flight, but seated correctly. After realizing the error and discovering that the flight she should have been on had already departed, she was told she could take the next flight. She refused to accept that and persistently pleaded that she needed to get on her flight. She reminded them that she was visually impaired, and she had her transportation set up for that flight's arrival. She continued to insist that she must get on that plane.

After a while, the attendant told her that she must be very important because the plane was coming back. We know the airline is governed by strict FAA guidelines; this just doesn't happen. But it did happen! Deep within I was thinking how God is everywhere, all the time, and all at the same time. When that sister said in spite of all the turmoil, she made it to her destination on time as if nothing happened. I broke out in a shout like a mad woman! That day my deliverance came. I was set free from shyness and shame and have been to this very day! Since then, I have worked the alter for two mega ministry pastors. Over 6,000 people were there, I was not ashamed to lay hands on and pray with them during the alter call. God said that we overcome by the Blood of the Lamb and the words of our testimony.

I am a witness, God is continuing to use my dear friends, Bishop Robert and Pastor Patricia Hunt of Wise Virgin Ministries, Palmetto, Florida mightily. People are being blessed because of the prayers of the righteous. I have seen them online praying for people until almost 12 a.m. They never, ever ask for money. This is the Clarion Call to righteousness. We must always walk circumspectly. As we do, surely the Lord will be our Shepard. The Lord is my Shepard.

Chapter 9

Miracles, Signs, and Wonders

I dedicate this chapter to *Miracles, Signs, Wonders,* and answered ridiculous prayers. Miracles, signs, and wonders are more readily understood to be within the realm of God's amazing working power. While some may wonder what are answered *ridiculous* prayers and ridiculous favor. Well, it's when you pray asking God for what would appear to be a ridiculous or impossible request. Oh, but God!

You'll see exactly what I mean in the following events, which I experienced firsthand or came into the knowledge of through the testimony of the one who personally experienced it. I have seen what many would not believe. These events are not given in any chronological order, they are being shared with you as Lord recalls them in me.

I recall the time we were in Tampa, Florida visiting. I had just purchased a new Chrysler Town and Country Van. If I'm not mistaken, it had seven miles on it when we bought it. At the time of the trip, we'd only had it a few months. After saying goodbye to relatives, we left my sister's house heading back home. As we approached the first red light, the vehicle began to malfunction. My husband was driving, he said he knew what the problem was, all he needed was some help to fix it. Immediately, I thought of something that I heard my pastor say at House of Prayer. So, I said, "In the name of Jesus I call you in the spirit, I command you to come to this location, right now, in the name of Jesus!" In about five minutes the person I was asking God to send showed up at the stop light, right where my new vehicle was broken down.

On another occasion, it was a Sunday evening, and we didn't have service. I was watching a Christian show, when the Lord spoke to me and said, 'You are just as anointed as Juanita Bynum or T.D Jakes.' I thought, what! I immediately called my sister and asked her what she thought about that. She said, "I think you are." I trusted my sister, still I sought another opinion. I got the same response. Soon after, Evangelist Linda Oliver, a sister from Syracuse, NY came to visit our church, she mentioned that her pastor, Bishop Robert W. Jones of Apostolic Church of Jesus Christ, was having a convention and needed alter workers. I, among others, agreed to go to the convention. In the end, I was the only one that went to Syracuse, NY. It was a two-night revival; the guest speakers were Bishop Noel Jones and Bishop T.D. Jakes. During the alter call, we laid hands on many to receive the Holy Ghost. God watches over His Word to perform it.

One day, while sitting at my desk at work, I heard the Lord say that most of my money will come from my tapes and books. I was thinking to myself, how. I'm not big and I don't know anyone that is. Before I could finish that thought, the telephone rang. I wasn't in a rush to answer, when I looked at the caller ID, it said MALACO RECORDS. I'm thinking, what! My mind was racing over the singers signed to that label as I quickly answered the phone. The lady said, "Hello, my name is Mary Jennings and I need to speak with Brother D." I told her, "Ma'am you have the wrong number, but you do have the right number!" I went on to tell her what the Lord had just told me. She said, "Yes, this is the Lord." She was the kindest, sweetest person you would ever want to speak with. I could easily say that she called me by mistake, but I know it was God working strategically and He will show Himself. Now, here it is over twenty plus years later and I'm writing, and you are reading my first book! God is God alone!

I remember the time a woman of faith at my church prayed with me concerning a court hearing being held before an Administrative Law Judge. The thought occurred to me that I would have to wait for a decision. So, I changed my prayer and asked God to allow me to know the outcome before I left the hearing. After the hearing was called to order, the judge says, "On this date, I have before me... and proceeds to name everyone and states a few other things. The judge addresses me regarding where I've worked, to which I answer, "Yes, Sir." I was thinking, when is my attorney going to say something. The judge said that he could see that I was not a lazy person. He then asked my attorney if he had anything to say. My attorney was puzzled. He spoke a few word in my defense. The judge then stated that in lieu of the evidence that he had before him and my testimony, that he found in favor of me!! You all do know this just doesn't happen! You would normally have to wait thirty days to get a determination letter, if not longer. God is faithful!

Listen, when you've booked your flight, prepared to have assistance because you're legally blind, and you've received your pastor's blessing for your trip, you think you've done everything to make sure things go off without a hitch. Right? This is the testimony of a dear church sister. She was dependent on the flight attendants to get her properly boarded on her flight; it was their job. But when she got to her seat someone was already seated in it. Now, both passengers were right about it being their seat, the only problem was, she was on the wrong plane. Her plane was already enroute to its destination, and even with flight attendant assistance, she was somehow left behind. She persistently pleaded her case with the attendants, telling them that they must get her on that plane. Yes, she was asking them to get her on a plane that was already in the air! Do you hear the ridiculous prayer, the impossible prayer starting? She told them they had to get her on that plane because her transportation was set to pick her up at the time of that flight's arrival. She also reminded them that she was legally blind. She was told, she would be put on the next flight, but she refused to accept that option. A short while later an attendant came and told her, "You must be a very special person, because the plane is coming back!" Her plane came back! She was seated on the very plane that left without her just as she declared and decreed that she would be. Yes! The plane that left without her, returned to get her, and it arrived at its destination as scheduled as if nothing happened. That's *answered ridiculous prayer* and FAVOR. I know, we've heard it said that favor isn't fair, but oh YES, it is fair because it's of God!

In the book of St. Matthew Jesus taught the people, he never taught the church. He said if you ask any thing in my name, I will do it. (John 14:14) Faith is what moves God. All you need is faith the size of a mustard seed; He's no respecter of person. The fact that you ask is mustard-seed faith.

Please understand, if you can supply the faith, God will supply the ridiculousness. God did it with Moses at the Red Sea, He did it with me in court, He did it with Lazarus in the tomb. Just recently, He did it with me in Kroger's parking lot. God will do it for you. Yes! Oh, yes, He will! We cannot live good enough to deserve anything from God, it's only by His grace and mercy that we all are not consumed. I double dog dare you to have just a little faith and ask in expectation; God will do it according to His will.

CPSIA information can be obtained
at www.ICGtesting.com
Printed in the USA
LVHW081823211122
733724LV00016B/1345

9 781955 107778